Understanding the Koran

Understanding the Koran

A Quick Christian Guide to the Muslim Holy Book

Mateen Elass

ZONDERVAN™

GRAND RAPIDS, MICHIGAN 49530 USA

We want to hear from you. Please send your comments about this book to us in care of zreview@zondervan.com. Thank you.

ZONDERVAN™

Understanding the Koran
Copyright © 2004 by Mateen Elass

Requests for information should be addressed to:

Zondervan, *Grand Rapids, Michigan 49530*

Library of Congress Cataloging-in-Publication Data
Elass, Mateen, 1955-
    Understanding the Koran : a quick Christian guide to the Muslim holy book / Mateen Elass.
       p. cm.
    Includes indexes.
    ISBN-10: 0-310-24812-4
    ISBN-13: 978-0-310-24812-5
    1. Koran--Relation to the Bible. 2. Islam — Relations--Christianity. 3. Christianity and other religions--Islam. 4. Koran--Criticism, interpretation, etc. 5.Koran--Controversial literature. I. Title.
BP134.B4E43 2004
297.1'2261'02423--dc22

                 2004002229
                 CIP

Interior design by Lori Vezina

Printed in the United States of America

---

07 08 09 10 /❖ DC/ 10 9 8 7 6

C O N T E N T S

The Koran through Muslim Eyes

wice a day, the cannon shot echoed across our town. It was
Ramadan, the ninth month of the Islamic calendar. My family
lived in Saudi Arabia, and the artillery booms marked the officially
determined times of dawn and sunset, between which all practicing
Muslims were to fast from food, drink, and other pleasures.

Saudi Arabia is a self-described Muslim nation and, as such, pro-
mulgates and enforces the teachings of the Islamic prophet Muhammad
as found in the Koran.[1] Fasting during the month of Ramadan is one of
many of these practices. Since it is commanded in the Koran, it is
enjoined on all faithful Muslims. Why? Because for the Muslim the
Koran is the Word of God, the highest authority on earth by which to
regulate one's life. It is their Holy Book, and it plays a role in Islam in
many ways similar to that of the Bible in Christianity. Yet there are also
many significant differences, and the task of this book is to help those
unfamiliar with the Koran to become conversant enough with it and its
place in Islamic society to compare and contrast it with the Bible and its
use in Christian contexts. I also hope that by the time you finish reading this book, you will have increased confidence in conversing about
faith issues with Muslims you may encounter in daily life or travels.

A Growing Number of Muslims

Islam claims over 1.2 billion adherents worldwide, second in size and scope only to Christianity, which numbers roughly 1.9 billion. Together, these two religions account for almost half the world's population. Amazingly, they remain relatively ignorant of each other's central beliefs. Though the reasons for this are no doubt complex, they should not continue, at least not for the Western Christian world. For many years, Islam has seemed to the Christian West to be a religion of the Middle East and other Third World nations. Having little direct contact with Muslims, most Christians remain ignorant of this world religion. But because of the influx of Muslim immigrants to Europe and North America, the rise of militant Islam and its attendant terrorist targeting of Western interests, and the reopening of painful wounds in the Israeli-Palestinian conflict, Islam is very much in the forefront of media interest. Issues of style of dress, special dietary rules, different days of worship, and stringent religious practices are all contributing to a new curiosity among Americans as to the nature and beliefs of Islam.

Christians can no longer afford to be indifferent to the teachings and practices of this faith birthed in the seventh-century Arabian Peninsula, which now finds its home in the bulk of Asia and Africa and is quickly making inroads into Europe and the United States. If the church is to be serious about its commission to make disciples of all people groups, then we must be conversant with the belief system that presently sways one fifth of the world's population. Perhaps the quickest way to do this well is to familiarize ourselves with the Koran, which stands at the heart of Muslim theology and practice.

A Unique Physical Book

For the Muslim, there is no book on earth that is its equal. Roughly the size of the New Testament, it claims to be the revelation of Allah (God) to Muhammad in the language of Arabic. Native Arabic speakers recognize a beauty and power in the poetic diction of the Koran, which some claim has never been equaled in the history of human communication.

For this reason, as well as because of the theological place of the Koran in the Arab Muslim world, Koranic Arabic has become the standard for what is now known as classical Arabic, the primary dialect of the educated and refined throughout the Middle East.

Since Muslims consider the Koran to be the literal words of God (i.e., spoken directly from the mouth of God through the angel Gabriel to Muhammad, who then repeated these exact words to his listeners, who in turn memorized or transcribed them), the physical book itself becomes an object of holy veneration. There are particular rules for how it is to be handled and treated. For example, in elementary schools in Saudi Arabia, children are taught to wash themselves and be in a state of ritual purity before handling the Koran, to kiss it three times before opening it to read, and then to kiss it again three times and touch it to one's forehead after closing it and putting it away. Menstruating women must not touch it. The Koran is not to be left open and unattended, lest the devil or a *jinn* come along and read it (presumably, their unclean

presence would greatly dishonor it, and their increased knowledge of Allah's Word would enable them to cause more mischief).

As a sign of its ultimate value, the Koran is to occupy the highest place in a home or mosque, above all other books or objects. Hence it should be on the highest bookshelf in the house, with nothing sitting above it. When held, it is never to be carried below the waistline. When transported among belongings in a suitcase, it is to be the last thing packed so as not to be covered by anything else. It is never to be placed on the ground, lest one incur the wrath of Allah. Often, however, the Koran is read by those seated on the floor prior to prayer. For such individuals there are special book holders that allow the book to rest open and off the ground. It is a great dishonor and embarrassment to allow the Koran to fall to the earth.

I remember a story, perhaps apocryphal, that circulated throughout the Middle East in the early 1970s about one of the earliest African-American athletes to convert to Islam. Desiring to learn more of the faith he had embraced, he accepted an invitation to tour the holy sites of Islam in Saudi Arabia. His presence caused a great stir of excitement among Arab Muslims in Mecca and Medina. Dressed in Saudi robes and carrying a Koran, he cut quite a figure among the admirers surrounding him. Asked for his autograph, he found a chair on which to sit, and then very naturally tucked his Koran under the chair legs so as to be out of the way while he signed papers. Immediately, the bustle around him ceased with stunned and embarrassed silence. When one of his handlers recognized what had happened, he quickly retrieved the Koran, brushed it off and kissed it, and apologized profusely to his fellow Muslims on behalf of the athlete, who after all hadn't known any better.

Though somewhat mollified, the crowds no longer thronged about this famous American; indeed, as word spread, disrespect mounted and the extended tour had to be cut short. While I cannot confirm that this particular event actually happened, the story certainly rings true in terms of typical Muslim reactions to perceived indifference to or disrespect for "the Noble Koran." No human being, no matter how popular or respected, is of greater importance than the Koran. Those who dishonor it will face the indignation of good Muslims everywhere.

Punishment for Abuse of the Book

Of even greater import for Muslims, however, is the belief that Allah will protect his book and will punish infidels who attempt to abuse it. The Koran itself contains many references to the dire fate of those who disbelieve Muhammad's claims and make fun of his teachings. These unbelievers will be undone in the fires of hell, while God's revelation remains protected.

Stories abound in the Muslim world today of attempts to dishonor the Koran that have been foiled by the supernatural power of God. One of my cousins related to me an account from her childhood in Saudi Arabia. It was said that an infidel (opponent of Islam) had broken into the home of a Muslim family to cause mischief. Finding a copy of the Koran while ransacking the place, he threw it into the toilet—an act of horrific desecration in Muslim eyes. When the family arrived home and saw the damage to their home, they were naturally downcast. Upon finding their Koran in the toilet, they were mortified. Quickly fishing it out to see if it could be rescued, they were astonished to discover that though it had lain completely submerged in water, it was not in the least bit wet. God had fully protected his noble book. This story parallels a declaration found in the Hadith traditions:[2] "If the Koran were wrapped in a skin and thrown into a fire, it would not burn" (Al-Tirmidhi, 652).

While most educated Muslims do not take such stories at face value, to the less educated masses such supernatural interventions concerning the Koran are par for the course. The underlying presupposition is that the honor of Allah is closely tied to the honor of this book, and that he will do whatever is needed to defend his honor. For this reason as well, since Muslims proclaim that the Koran is without error of any kind, having as its source the perfect mind of God, most are not open to examining its contents critically. Forbidden questions would be:

- What pre-Koranic sources influenced Muhammad?

- Since the Koran recognizes the full inspiration of the Bible, why are there serious discrepancies at points between what it says and what Muhammad teaches?
- How did the Koran come to be in the form in which we find it today?

These questions are seen as dishonoring to God and his prophet. The answer, quite simply, is that God spoke everything to Muhammad; nothing came from the prophet's own thinking. The words of God were perfectly preserved and collected before the prophet's death, and the Koran today is exactly the same as it was when it was first presented to the world almost fourteen centuries ago. If there are discrepancies between the Koran and the Bible, that is the fault of Jews and Christians, who perverted the truth they originally received. The Koran, by God's perfect wisdom and power, restores and clarifies the truth as it was originally given to Moses and Jesus. To seek to delve behind the revealed words of the Koran is to disbelieve their divine source and so to dishonor Allah. For the faithful Muslim, this must not be done.

Its Self-Proclaimed Exalted Status

Not surprisingly, the Koran often speaks of its own exalted status. Since Muhammad was opposed early by many who claimed that his revelations were counterfeit, a significant number of his messages are defensive in nature, claiming an exalted, divine status. Early commentators listed fifty-five titles given the Koran in its pages. Though many of these are redundant, a sample will demonstrate the place Muhammad expected it to play in the lives of his followers:

• Establisher of Truth	• Sermon
• Enlightener	• Message
• Reminder	• Narrative
• Straight Path	• Wisdom
• Explanation	• Philosopher

The above titles all emphasize the Koran's claim to be the ultimate conduit of a true picture of God, humanity, and the world. This picture is held to be in line with all of God's previous revelations, including that found in the Bible. Muhammad's interest in setting the Koran on a par with the Old and New Testaments is underscored by two biblical titles given it: the Psalm and the Herald of Good Tidings.

But the Muslim Scriptures are not simply an essay on Truth; they seek to change the lives of those who hear the message. The Koran is a hortatory book, exhorting humanity to obedience to the Sovereign One and laying out what this means in no uncertain terms. Titles such as the Guide, the Righteous, the Justice, the Exhortation, the Warner, the Order, the Firm Handle, the Distinguishing Speech, and the Health all serve to underscore the goal of moral obedience inherent in these teachings.

Other titles stressing the unique qualities of the Koran set it apart from mere human works. It is called each of the following:

• The Good	• The Mighty
• The Inspiration	• The Uniform
• The Wonderful	• The Lofty
• The Exalted	• The Blessed
• The Excellent	• The Proof
• The Purified	• The Mercy
• The Light	

Such names emphasize the eternal and divine nature claimed for itself and demand that all who hear its message bow before its unmatchable stature and beauty. Muslims frequently claim that there is no book on earth that can match the Koran in terms of literary power and elegance. In Muhammad's day the challenge was frequently issued to opponents to try and formulate their own poetry to match the creative genius recognized in Koranic Arabic. Not surprisingly, non-Muslim Arabic speakers claim there are many early Arabic works that equal or exceed portions of the Koran, while Muslims categorically deny this possibility. Beauty, indeed, is in the eye of the beholder!

In conversations, Muslims most often refer to their Scriptures as the "Glorious Koran" or the "Noble Koran." Within the last century, as Muslims have become more familiar with Christian claims about the Bible and its traditional title as the "Holy Bible," some have applied this title to the Koran, especially in English translations. Though the adjective "holy" is not found in the Koran as a self-description, there is no doubt that the idea is derivable from the other titles found there. In a shorthand fashion, Muslims sometimes speak of the Koran as *al-Furqan* ("the Distinguisher"), *Kalimat Allah* ("the Word of God"), or simply *al-Kitab* ("the Book").

Learning at an Early Age

During a young Muslim's educational years, much time is spent learning portions of the Koran by heart. Emphasis is placed not only on memorizing the texts but also learning the correct pronunciation of the Arabic words. Naturally, in non-Arabic-speaking countries this is of critical importance. Since the recitation of Koranic texts is a core element of the Muslim prayer ritual, and since these prayers must be said in Arabic, the correct intonation of the scriptural texts is essential. Sadly, many Third-World Muslims do not understand the words they speak in prayer, though they know in their own tongues the gist of what they have learned by rote in Arabic language schools run by the local mosque.

In the Arab world, the Koran figures large in the typical school program, from elementary to college years. Studies in language and doctrine as well as in history, science, and the arts all sing the praise of the Koran and an Islamic worldview. By the time one graduates from a Muslim school system, he or she will have been exposed to rote repetition of the entire Koran. At Al-Azhar University in Cairo, the oldest continuously existing university in the world, one of the requirements for graduation is that each student must be prepared to successfully recite the entire Koran from memory.

Art and Geometric Patterns

While such a feat is not expected of all Muslims, the memorization of significant portions of the Koran is encouraged for all believers, as well as regular reading. One Hadith tradition declares, "The state of a Muslim who reads the Koran is like the orange fruit whose smell and taste are pleasant." Islamic societies are immersed in the pervasive influence of the Koran. Favorite texts are found dangling from taxi rearview mirrors, inscribed on jewelry, and laced throughout everyday conversations.

Islam has an uneasy relationship with art since Muhammad cursed artists who drew or painted human or animal forms (a reaction against the polytheism of his day). Hence, most artwork in Muslim culture derives from geometric patterns (such as mother of pearl and wood inlays found on backgammon boards, boxes, and furniture) or from the calligraphy of the Arabic language, whose flowing style lends itself effortlessly to intricate and breathtaking designs.

Naturally, the text of the Koran serves as the fundamental content for such ornamental calligraphy. Koranic calligraphic art is found in mosques; on public buildings; in prized, often ancient copies of the Koran; and at Islamic holy sites. In the homes of devout Muslims, where the ban on any human or animal images is maintained, framed scriptural quotations in colorful calligraphy are typical. On the wall in my office is one such piece of art that used to hang in my father's study. Written on parchment in blues and golds, with traces of red, the Arabic script almost dances with graceful curves and is intertwined with sleek, sharp lines and bold pointings. One does not have to be able to read Arabic to enjoy the beauty of this developed art form.

My Visit to Damascus and Memorization

Some Muslims make their livelihood from being reciters of the Koran at special family or social occasions. Last fall while in Damascus, I visited the Umayyad Mosque, located within the old city walls. The fourth holiest site in Islam after Mecca, Medina, and the Dome of the Rock in Jerusalem, this mosque is an impressive sight, containing among other relics the tomb of Saladin and a shrine said to hold the head of John the Baptist (who, interestingly, is a recognized prophet in Islamic tradition). As my guide took me around the mosque, we stopped before this shrine. It was surrounded by women, for tradition holds that those who touch its stone walls and pray there will be blessed with fertility, based apparently on the fact that John was conceived by a previously barren and also relatively old Elizabeth (see Luke 1:5–25 for the full account).

Near this particularly holy site, a group of six men were seated on Persian rugs, spaced about three feet apart and unconcerned with the bustle happening all around them. They were swaying gently forward and back as their mouths moved in quiet speech. I had woven my way through them without much notice when the guide asked me if I understood their purpose. I shook my head. "These men are all blind," he said. "They have memorized the Koran perfectly and spend their days at the mosque reciting it. People know they are here, and when they wish to hear the Koran recited at weddings or funerals or for special family occasions, they hire one of these *qurra'* (i.e., individuals who have memorized and can recite any portion of the Koran).

Such individuals are accorded great respect in Muslim society. Even greater in esteem are those who have memorized the Koran and become acknowledged interpreters of its message. One Hadith tradition relates, "The best person among you is he who has learned the Koran and teaches it" (al-Bukhari, 6.545). The religious teacher is expected to have labored long and hard over the meaning of the words of Allah, to devote all his energies to knowing it intimately. So another tradition declares, "He who is an expert in the Koran shall rank with the 'Honored Righteous Scribes,' and he who reads the Koran with difficulty and gets tired over it [i.e., expends much honorable effort] shall receive double rewards" (al-Bukhari, 6.459). Even everyday conversations among Muslim acquaintances are peppered with quotations from the Koran to support conclusions. In public debates the better versed one is in the Koran, the more verbally powerful his or her arguments are accepted to be.

Nevertheless, the gulf in perspective and knowledge between such a scholar and the typical Muslim on the street is often huge. While Muhammad's followers all revere the Koran as most holy and exalted, there is a fine line that, when crossed at the popular level, turns the Koran into a source of magical powers or an object of worship itself. Particularly in folk Islam, where Muslim beliefs are interwoven with animistic superstitions, the Koran is viewed as a powerful aid in the battle against evil forces. Often talismans (known as *ta'wiz*) are worn on the body of the superstitious Muslim. Constructed typically of a black cord or some other cloth, the talisman will have woven or sewn into it a piece of metal on which a Koranic text has been inscribed. Similarly, Muslims sometimes wear around their neck or waist, or on the arm, a gold or silver case with a scroll of scriptural text inside. These objects are held to ward off evil spirits, to deflect curses or "the evil eye" of others, and to be of aid in physical and psychic healing.

Another common practice may be called the "ingesting of the Word." When someone is ill or in danger or wandering from the straight path, verses from the Koran are sometimes written with ink or sandalwood paste on the inside of a bowl or plate. Water is then poured into the dish to dissolve the writing, and this water is then given to the "patient" to drink.

I learned a few months ago of a variation on this practice used by a Muslim immigrant family in Chicago. The traditional grandmother, deeply concerned about the unhealthy social influences surrounding her granddaughter in this country and her increasing Americanization, wrote out on paper some verses of the Koran reputed to be very powerful in their spiritual influence, then placed the paper in a glass, filled it with water, and let it sit until the ink had dissolved. When the girl in question returned home from school that day, the grandmother insisted she drink the cup dry. Only in this way, by having the sacred words ingested literally into her body, could this young teenage girl find strength to remain true to the tenets of Islam.

In all fairness it must be said that superstitious Christians sometimes view the Bible in much the same way. In my late teenage years I knew a devout young lady who had been raised in the Bible Belt. One autumn day she came down with a sore throat, which increasingly bothered her. The next day, however, she felt fine, and attributed this to the fact that when she had gone to bed the night before she had placed an open Bible over her neck, and that God through that means had healed her. Superstitious use of holy objects is not limited to any one religion.

As Christians look to the Bible for specific direction and guidance in life, so Muslims appeal to the Koran. Those who do not know very well the contents of their respective holy books often use the same method for seeking God's will at a critical juncture of their lives. After praying for guidance, they will open up the Scriptures at random and, without peeking, will place the index finger somewhere on the open page. Hoping God is somewhere in the mix, sovereignly overseeing their actions, they will then read the passage on which their finger fell and attempt to justify it (if at all possible) as God's will for them in this situation. Both Muslim and Christian clerics decry this practice, but it goes on at the popular level, indicating at least two things: the high level of ignorance among the masses as to what their respective holy books say about living according to God's will, and the deep hunger evident in religious people of all stripes to know and carry out that will.

The Day the Music Was Silenced

To understand the Muslim mind better, let me conclude this chapter by showing a contrast between the place of music with regard to the Koran and the Bible. In the Islamic world, holiness is associated with seriousness and sobriety. Thus, when the Koran is read publicly, whatever else has been going on in the environs must cease. Out of respect, everyone must listen, or give the appearance of listening, to the recitation. No music is allowed, even in the background, when the Koran is recited. Music is seen as entertainment or diversion and thus has no place in a holy setting where the Koran is proclaimed. To compensate for this, Islamic culture has created a kind of voice art utilized strictly for the public recitation of Koranic verses. Called *tartil*, this art uses ululation and other forms of voice modulation together with the elongation of various syllables to create the sing-song or chanting effect so familiar to the ears of any traveler in the Middle East. Nevertheless, Muslims do not consider this music.

Not long ago, my father, a lifelong Muslim, died suddenly at his home. When the unwelcome phone call came from my brother to break the news, thoughts raced through my mind, and my heart was filled with yearnings, regrets, and hopes for my father's eternal well-being. I was surprised to learn that the extended family was adamant that his burial should be in Syria. So we flew over a few days later. There at the public memorial reception in his honor, the services of a number of these skilled chanters were retained.

As we sat in relative silence, these chanters took turns reciting portions of the Koran. During breaks, soft, traditional music was played in the background. At one point during one of these breaks, a heated argument broke out. This break had occurred during evening prayers, and many mourners were heading to the mosque adjoining the hall we had rented for the reception. The argument centered on the fact that the Koran was being recited next door, and it was inappropriate for any music to be played. Others responded that there were no recitations going on in our hall, so it was all right. The more conservative interpretation won the day.

For the Muslim, then, holiness and the vast array of human emotions do not mix. Prayer times at the mosque are somber, subdued affairs. Typical Islamic worship does not include music of any sort. How different from the Christian world, whose Scripture includes an inspired songbook (the Psalms) within its canon! For Jews and Christians, holiness certainly demands weightiness and the seriousness that attends anything profound. Nevertheless, holiness also demands joy, for the thrice-holy God is also the wellspring of all blessing. At the heart of his being is joy, and in his presence all is well. As C. S. Lewis was fond of saying, "Joy is the serious business of heaven."

It is no wonder, then, that Christians down through our history have employed music as a conduit for expressing the full range of our emotions in worship, especially our praise and adoration of God and our joy at being the objects of his redeeming love. The Bible in particular provides the content, directly or indirectly, for the hymn texts set to music. Far from feeling that the Scriptures are too holy to be combined with music, the Christian argues that at times music of the appropriate style and form supplementing the revealed truth of Scripture is the only vehicle that can adequately express our devotion to the full holiness of the One in whom we believe.

Two different holy books, with two widely divergent ways of using them in worship. If the Bible is inspired by God, how can the Koran make the same claim? Where did the Koran come from? How did Muhammad arrive at his claims of revelation? Why are Muslims so captivated by the Arabic form and structure of this text? To these questions about the Arabian prophet and his book we now turn.

Where Did the Koran Come From?

Three years ago, a Syrian relative shared with me her experience of traveling to Medina after performing the Hajj in Mecca. She went to pay her respects at the tomb of Muhammad. Her eyes filled with tears as she described the overwhelming sense of gratitude and devotion she felt toward Muhammad for his faithfulness and example as the Prophet of Allah. Without him, she believed, there would be no clear word from Allah about how she should live her life, and she would be spiritually impoverished.

The Koran and Muhammad share a symbiotic relationship. It is all but impossible to discuss the one without in some way including the other. So, to adequately discuss the origins of the Koran, we must look at the life of Muhammad and his claims to be a prophet of God in the same lineage as the prophets of the Old and New Testaments. Where does the story begin?

An Orphan

Born around A.D. 570 among the powerful Quraish tribe of Mecca, Muhammad soon became an orphan. His father died just months before his birth, and his mother passed away in his sixth year of life. Taken under the protective care of an influential uncle, Abu Talib,

Muhammad was raised in the mercantile business—not an unusual career in the trade capital of the Arabian peninsula. Though not much is known of his youth, Muslim sources report that at age twelve Muhammad traveled with his uncle to Syria—one of numerous caravan trips Muhammad took. Undoubtedly, during such excursions he came into contact with the great monotheistic religions rooted in the Middle East, Christianity and Judaism. The stark contrasts between their teachings and practices and those of his pagan tribe and its neighbors could not have failed to register with the young seeker.

She Proposes Marriage

Apparently successful as a tradesman and with a reputation for honesty (in his pre-prophetic days, he had been nicknamed *al-Amin*, "the trustworthy one"), Muhammad was hired at age twenty-five to manage the business affairs of a wealthy widow named Khadijah. Though fifteen years his elder, Khadijah fell in love with Muhammad and proposed marriage. He accepted, and they enjoyed twenty-five years of faithful married life before she died. It was only after Khadijah's death that Muhammad began to practice polygamy, marrying up to eleven wives, but Khadijah always retained an inviolable place in his heart.

Khadijah was the one who reassured Muhammad when at age forty he began hearing voices and seeing visions. For years he had taken private retreats to caves on Mount Hira outside Mecca for meditation and quietude. One day, he returned home in consternation, for he had encountered a supernatural being in a dream. Fearing he might be possessed by an evil spirit or starting on the path to becoming a despised soothsayer, he sought assurance from both his wife and his close cousin Waraqa. Muslim sources report this defining event of Muhammad's life:

> . . . one day the revelation came down to him, and the angel came to him and said, "Read"; but the Prophet said, "I am not a reader." And the Prophet related that the angel took hold of him, and squeezed him as much as he could bear, and then said again, "Read"; and the Prophet said, "I am not a reader." Then the angel

took hold of him a second time, and squeezed him as much as he could bear, and then let him go, and said, "Read"; then the Prophet said, "I am not a reader." Then the angel again seized the Prophet, and squeezed him, and said:

> "Read thou, in the name of thy Lord who created;
>   Created man out of clots of blood:
> Read thou! For thy Lord is the most Beneficent, Who hath taught the use of the pen;
>   Hath taught man that which he knoweth not."

Then the Prophet repeated the words with a trembling heart. And he returned to Khadijah, and said, "Wrap me up, wrap me up." And they wrapped him up in a garment until his fear was dispelled; and he told Khadijah what had occurred, and he said to Khadijah, "I was afraid I should die." Then Khadijah said, "No, it will not be so, I swear by God. He will never make thee melancholy or sad. For you are kind to your relatives, you speak the truth, you are faithful in trust, you bear the afflictions of the people, you spend in good works what you gain in trade, you are hospitable, and you assist your fellow men."[1]

A significant gap of time ensued between this first vision and subsequent heavenly visits, during which Muhammad grew greatly depressed, fearing that God either hated or had forsaken him. The Hadith of al-Bukhari (9:111) records that during this time span, Muhammad contemplated suicide by throwing himself off a cliff. Finally, however, the angel is said to have returned and addressed the fledgling prophet again, "O thou enwrapped in thy mantle, arise and preach." Further instruction from this encounter is found in Sura[2] 74. Encouraged, Muhammad began to develop a new identity as an apostle of the One True God, commissioned to call his idolatrous people to repentance and to knowledge and service of Allah. His Meccan tribesmen must acknowledge his prophetic mantle and submit in obedience, thereby choosing heaven over hell and preparing well for the coming Day of Judgment.

Opposition to His Message

Over the first ten years, Muhammad's message met much resistance. Mecca, after all, was the Wal-Mart Supercenter of idol worship, and bashing polytheism had grave economic as well as religious consequences. Though a few of Muhammad's family and friends rallied around him, the majority of the Quraish denounced him and began persecuting the movement.

The problem was not in the call to accept Allah as the Supreme Being—the Quraish were willing to concede that point. In fact, the great God Allah was given the title "Lord of the Kaʾaba [the central shrine of Mecca]." But Muhammad would not allow for any junior partners; all lesser gods had to go. The Koran specifically names three goddesses believed by the Quraish to serve as intercessors for them (53:19–22). They were known popularly as the daughters of Allah, but Muhammad attacked this belief by utilizing the cultural chauvinism of his day to say that if Allah were to have any offspring at all, he certainly would choose sons over daughters. The fact that he does not have any sons precludes the possibility of there being any daughters of Allah. The Quraish responded with intensified persecution.

Death in the Family and His Flight

During this trying period, both Khadijah and Abu Talib (Muhammad's wife and his protector) passed away, dealing the prophet a severe emotional blow. He began to despair of life in Mecca, so left with his adopted son Zaid to preach for the first time in the nearby town of Taif. To say his message was not received well would be an understatement—they were stoned and then run out of town. But in the following year, Muhammad's fortunes began to change. During the annual pagan pilgrimage to Mecca, he met six men from the town of Yathrib (two hundred miles north of Mecca), who embraced his teachings and agreed to spread them back home.

Within two years, seventy men from Yathrib had pledged their lives to Muhammad and his protection. When the Quraish, Muhammad's tribal clan, discovered Muhammad's success in Medina, they sensed his potential threat to their status quo and plotted to kill him. Muhammad, however, escaped from town and, after hiding two days in a cave with Abu Bakr, fled to Yathrib safely on June 20, 622. The event of this date became known as the *Hijrah* ("flight, migration"), which serves as the beginning of the Muslim calendar.

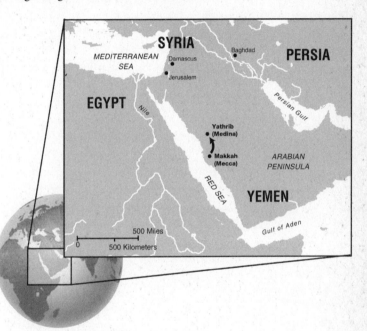

Muhammad and his following grew strong in Yathrib, which he renamed Medinat al-Nabi ("city of the prophet"), later shortened simply to Medina. As followers gathered round him from various tribes, they abandoned their former tribal allegiances and formed a new social unit (known as the *ummah*, i.e., "the community"), based on a new primary loyalty to Allah, his Messenger, and all true believers. It was here they proudly took on themselves the name Muslims ("the submitters").

Receiving Revelations in Medina

While the majority of Muhammad's revelations in the early Meccan period were relatively short, poetic, and focused on the message of strict monotheism, his revelations in Medina became increasingly long, pedestrian, and devoted to the social, political, and military details associated with developing a growing community amidst hostile parties. Medina was home to three Jewish tribes, who rejected Muhammad's claims to prophethood, ridiculed him, and sought his downfall. Muhammad's response was to banish two tribes from the city and massacre the third. He then turned his sights back to Mecca, desiring to conquer the city (peacefully, if possible) and to institute Islam as the sole religion of the holy city. Within ten years of his flight from Mecca, he returned in triumph, banished idols and their worship, and instituted many of the ritual practices of the Hajj pilgrimage, which continue to this day.

All through his life from age forty, Muhammad continued to receive revelations. There was never a sense that Allah had finished speaking until Muhammad unexpectedly died, and with his death came the end of Allah's words to the world. It was clear to his followers that Muhammad had served as the only conduit of revelation in their day and as the final prophet of the ages. There would be no further material to be gathered into the Koran.

A Miracle Book

Muslims believe the Koran to be divinely inspired like no book before or since its compilation. It is considered a miracle of perfect language and truth, given to the world through one "unlettered" and therefore incapable of devising it himself. Muhammad is said to have pointed to the revelations granted him as a compelling sign of his prophethood, since religious tradition taught that every true prophet could work miracles. Having no other miracles in his corner, Muhammad argued with his Meccan opponents that the Koran was his one miracle and that because of its import such a miracle was enough.

Skeptics, however, were full of charges that his "revelations" were invented or borrowed with slight alterations from other sources, and Muhammad was sensitive to these attacks. In the Koran itself we find a defense, coming presumably from the lips of Allah, in support of Muhammad's integrity (though, of course, Muhammad is the one doing the reporting of what Allah supposedly said to him—see 9:16; 10:39; 11:16; 52:34; also 4:94; 53:4).

The Night of Power

Most Muslims consider the earthly Arabic Koran to be a perfect copy of an uncreated heavenly original. Though the material Korans they hold in their hands are, of course, created objects of ink, paper, and glue, the content of what they carry is eternal in essence. Since Allah's word is uncreated, its meaning is also uncreated. There is debate over whether the eternal book itself is written in Arabic, in which case Arabic is seen as the native language of heaven, or whether Allah translated it into Arabic, from which it was copied down by noble, righteous scribes in heaven (80:15) and then sent down complete to the lowest heaven.

The anniversary of this monumental event is known as "the night of power," a mysterious event celebrated in the Islamic calendar of holy days toward the end of the month of Ramadan. Because the night of power occurs during Ramadan, the whole month is charged with special meaning. Many Muslims attempt to recite the entire Koran over these thirty days. Though no one is said to know the exact date of the night of power, except the prophet Muhammad and perhaps a few of his closest companions, most Muslims commemorate it on the twenty-seventh day of Ramadan. The Koran declares this night to be of greater value than a thousand months and filled with blessing for all Muslims, for it memorializes the sending of Allah's very words to earth.

According to tradition, it was this heavenly Arabic Koran that the angel Gabriel transmitted in piecemeal fashion over time to Muhammad. In the Koran itself, Muhammad's revelations were said to be taken from a "well-guarded tablet" (85:21), the "mother of the scripture" (43:3) kept

27

hidden from the touch of all but the pure (56:76). For the typical Arab Muslim, the belief in a heavenly Koran in Arabic leads rather seamlessly to the proud view that Arabic is the language of heaven, and thus the Arab peoples have been favorably set apart by God. The fact that the five daily prayers of Islam must be learned and said in Arabic by all converts, regardless of whether they know Arabic, underscores the centrality of the language in the life of Islam. This requirement is because Koranic Arabic is the language of revelation, and much of the ritual prayers involve the correct quotation of passages from the Koran.

Can Translations Be Trusted?

Likewise, today's Muslims do not consider translations of the Koran into other languages to be the true Koran, for the revelatory message and the Arabic language are inseparable. Hence, translations are designated as interpretations and therefore inherently less reliable than the Arabic text. Translations approved by Islamic councils are never printed solely in the non-Arabic reader's language, but always with the Arabic text by its side on the same or facing page.

The Muslim world uniformly believes that Muhammad truly received heavenly revelations. Less consensus exists on the agency and mode of these revelations. The Muslim "man on the street" holds that the angel Jibril (Gabriel) was the divine agent who brought the messages to Muhammad, speaking them with such power and beauty as to inscribe the words perfectly on the prophet's heart. Therefore when the young prophet came back from his heavenly encounter to the people, he could speak without error the words learned in the presence of Gabriel. His followers then copied down the latest revelations on whatever was at hand: palm fronds, bones, paper, or even stone, so as to maintain a written record. These ultimately were gathered into the one book now known as the Koran.

The Role of Gabriel and the Holy Spirit

Yet neither the Koran nor the traditions are that simplistic. Only once in the Muslim holy book itself is Gabriel named as the medium of inspiration for Muhammad's recitations (2:91). Sura 16:104, by contrast, speaks of God's revelation to Muhammad in this way: "Say, The Holy Spirit brought it down from thy Lord in truth." Other Koranic references are innocuously general: In 26:193, the "faithful spirit" brings the true message to Muhammad; in 53:5, the agent is "one terrible in power." The traditions most often speak of the heavenly messenger as an angel, sometimes called Gabriel, but often nameless. Since the Koran's explanation of Muhammad's revelatory encounters conflates the terms "angel" and "spirit" and identifies Gabriel and the Holy Spirit as performing the same mediatorial function, it seems clear that Muhammad confused the two and compressed what are two distinct entities in the Bible into one being.

This conclusion is further supported by the fact that the vast majority of Muslim commentators (from classical to modern day) use the names Gabriel and Holy Spirit as synonyms. Moreover, in Islamic literature, Gabriel is spoken of as "the Supreme Spirit," "the Honored Spirit," and "the Spirit of casting into." Some Christian scholars have hypothesized that Muhammad's view may have stemmed from a misunderstanding of Luke's birth narratives of Jesus, where the angel Gabriel served as the divine messenger to Mary (Luke 1:26) of her impending virgin conception: "The Holy Spirit will come upon you, and the power of the Most High will overshadow you. So the holy one to be born will be called the Son of God" (1:35). Muhammad or his sources may have unwittingly confused the messenger of the good news with the agent who subsequently brought the good news to pass, and then carried this confusion over to the descriptions of his own purported heavenly encounters.

One of Muhammad's favorite wives, Aisha, reports in the traditions that the prophet's initial revelations did not come through an angel at all but were sent through the medium of dreams: "The first revelations which the Prophet received were in true dreams; and he never dreamt but it came to pass regularly as the dawn of day" (Mishkat 24:5). Given the disclosure elsewhere in Islamic tradition that Muhammad's earliest prophetic experiences were filled with doubts about their source and even the fear that he might be possessed, the lack of clarity or certainty regarding the true agent of the Koran's contents is distressing to those seeking to weigh Islam's claims.

How Muhammad Received Revelation

Since there are multiple views about the agent(s) of inspiration in the creation of the Koran, it should come as no surprise that Muslims acknowledge a colorful variety of modes in which that inspiration was conveyed to Muhammad. The traditions record Aisha as reporting that sometimes Muhammad was enveloped in a brightness like the brightness of the morning, during which times Gabriel somehow communicated the will of God to the prophet. At other times, Muhammad apparently would hear the tinkling of a bell, through which he alone could discern the words that heaven's messenger was relaying.

These auditory experiences in particular were said to be physically and emotionally overwhelming to the prophet; when the ringing reached his ears, his whole body would become agitated, and he would perspire profusely even in the wintertime. His normally glowing face would turn pasty and his head would be bowed with the weightiness of what he heard. If he happened to be riding a camel during such an episode, the camel itself would fall to the ground, presumably from the weight. Twice, the traditions say, angels with six hundred wings appeared as bearers of divine revelation. Moreover, Gabriel sometimes, though not in any bodily form, would invisibly inspire the heart of Muhammad so that the speech that came forth from his lips was none other than the utterance of God. In the midst of dreams, we are told, God would sometimes appear to Muhammad, place hands on his shoulders, and speak directly to the prophet.

But perhaps Muhammad's most exalted claim to a divine encounter through which he received revelation is tied to what has become known as the *Mi'raj* ("ascent"). Referred to in the Koran (17:1), this event is said to have taken place in the twelfth year of Muhammad's ministry: "Praise be to Him who carried His servant by night from the Masjid al-Haram [the sacred mosque of Mecca] to the Masjid al-Aqsa [the sacred mosque of Jerusalem]." Some Muslim scholars believe the *Mi'raj* to have been a vision, but most consider it to have been a literal trip. The traditions embellish this one Koranic reference by asserting that Muhammad's real ascent was not from Mecca to Jerusalem and back, but from Mecca to Jerusalem to heaven and back.

Indeed, the story goes that Muhammad was taken by a flying steed at Gabriel's side up to and through the first seven levels of heaven, at each point meeting some of the great prophets of history. At the highest level, Allah is said to have spoken to Muhammad directly, without the mediation of any angel. Here, the prophet received instructions concerning the divine requirements for the prayers of the faithful—all Muslims were to perform the rituals of prayer fifty times a day. Moses (residing in the sixth level of heaven) inquired of Muhammad what Allah had commanded of him, and after being told convinced Muhammad that the burden would be far too great for the people. He urged Muhammad to return to Allah and bargain on behalf of his people, which he did. After five bargaining sessions, the prayer requirement was reduced from fifty to five. Moses still thought this too many, but Muhammad said he was too ashamed to ask any further reductions, and so the number of mandatory prayers for the faithful stands at five.

A Perfect Book without Error?

As we learned in the previous chapter, Islam requires belief in the perfect transmission of truth from heaven to earth through the prophet Muhammad, all of which was gathered without error or omission after his death in the form of the Koran. This book, say the faithful, has not changed or been corrupted from the day it was fully compiled. Such a claim is apologetically necessary because of substantial conflicts between the Koran and the Bible on many different fronts. Since Muhammad had claimed earlier in his ministry that his God was identical with the God of biblical revelation, and that if his hearers had any questions about his revelations they should consult with the "people of the Book" (i.e., Jews and Christians) for clarification and support, the assumption naturally arose that what was revealed through Muhammad would interlock seamlessly with the revelations found in the Bible. When Christians and Jews began to take issue with some of Muhammad's teachings, and when further investigations uncovered significant differences between Koranic accounts of biblical events and those accounts from the Bible itself, the tensions between Muhammad's conflicting claims had to be resolved.

The Islamic solution was to conclude that since the Koran could not be wrong, the Bible must have become corrupted. Though originally it had affirmed the same truths as the Koran, over the years the teachings of Moses and David were perverted by unbelieving Jews, and the revelations of Jesus were twisted by unbelieving Christians. This approach enabled Muhammad and his followers to maintain that God had indeed once chosen the Jews and Christians as his people, but they had over time preferred to follow the whisperings of the devil and so polluted the truth with errors. Unwilling to repent by recognizing Muhammad as a prophet, they were now to be regarded as enemies of the faith or at least as deluded by the evil one.

Muhammad Made Corrections?

If God's revelation in the past was capable of being perverted, what was to prevent the same from occurring to the Koran? The Muslim's answer is that this time around, God through his angel spoke directly to the prophet, inscribing the words indelibly in his memory, which when subsequently reported to the people were copied down without error and kept secure. Hence, every syllable of the Koran is directly divine; there is no possibility for error to creep in. In the coming chapter we will see that the collection and transmission of Koranic material was not so simplistic. But we should note that the Koran does admit that Muhammad at times corrected some of his earlier revelations after discovering that he had somehow "gotten it wrong."

This occurs in two ways. At times Muhammad revealed material that contradicted earlier revelations. As a rationale, he claimed that Allah had abrogated the former and installed the latter as a "new and improved" version. So Sura 2:100 has Allah declaring, "If we abrogate a verse or consign it to oblivion, we offer something better than it or something of equal value." Astonishingly, Muhammad never seemed troubled by the inconsistency of affirming that the Koran is the perfect replica of the eternal book of God while at the same time declaring that at times God must reshape or annul earlier revelations.

But second and more troubling, Muhammad apparently at times unwittingly mixed truth and falsehood together in his report of God's revelations. He defended these missteps with the admission that even though he could unintentionally fall into error, God would not allow him to remain in error but would always send another revelation to correct faulty understanding.

The most famous among these incidents has become known as "the satanic verses," a phrase long known in Islam but made familiar to the West through Salman Rushdie's 1988 novel by that name. Although Rushdie's work is fictional and intended to satirize Islamic adherents and their practices rather than Muhammad and the Koran per se, the term "satanic verses" refers to an event in the life of the prophet widely reported in traditional Islamic sources.

In Muhammad's early prophetic days, when he faced opposition from his Meccan clan but had not yet been declared persona non grata, the prophet apparently looked for a way through compromise to win over the residents of the holy city. One day, as the chief leaders of the city were gathered beside the Ka'aba (even in pre-Islamic days revered as the holiest of shrines in Arabia) for their daily discussion of community issues, Muhammad showed up, seated himself innocuously in their midst, and began reciting what would become chapter 53 of the Koran. The revelation dealt with the status of three goddesses particularly esteemed by the Meccans: al-Lat, al-Uzza, and Manat. These idols were considered by the pagan Meccans to be daughters of the great god Allah and were worshiped as protectors of the city.

When Muhammad reached the point in his recitation where he framed the question, "What then do you think of al-Lat, and al-Uzza, and Manat, the third idol besides?" there was naturally great interest in the forthcoming answer. Joy erupted as he continued, "These are exalted females, and truly their intercession is to be hoped for." Here was a compromise they could live with. Allah would be recognized as the supreme god, but his daughters would still be acknowledged and offered due honor. Subsequently, however, when Muhammad's conventional followers heard this "revelation," they expressed their shock and disbelief that Muhammad could affirm something so contrary to his previous decrees.

Not surprisingly, within a short period of time, Muhammad brought a new revelation that corrected this error. The angel Gabriel, he said, gave him the "true reading" of this passage, in which the answer to the same question now read, "Shall you have male children and God female? Behold, this would be a most unjust division. Truly, these are merely names which you and your fathers have given them" (53:19–23).

Here the Meccans are upbraided not only for ascribing progeny to Allah, but especially for thinking that God might have (only) daughters while human beings could have sons. In the context of Arabian culture, where sons were prized and daughters merely tolerated, if not put to death at birth, this Koranic riposte is meant to shame the idolaters into repentance for their unworthy thoughts of God. The stringent monotheism of early Islam is reaffirmed, but at the expense of Muhammad's reputation as one who hears clearly from God.

The nagging question remains: If Muhammad could confidently report as revelation from Allah something that turned out to be (according to Islamic tradition itself) a perversion from Satan, how can one be certain that there are not further perversions that were not caught or corrected? The Muslim answer, of course, is that Allah has guarded his truth to prevent any error from remaining in the final recorded revelations. But this raises a further question: If God is so careful to protect the transmission of his truth through Muhammad into its final form in the Koran, why would he not have been equally careful to protect the truth he delivered through previous prophets?

In other words, why would he not have preserved the Bible, which Muslims now argue has been twisted because it teaches things contrary to the Koran? Either God has revealed himself most fully through Jesus Christ and the Bible (which serves as the primary, authoritative witness to him) or God has revealed himself most fully through the Koran. They cannot both be accepted as ultimate truth since they point in vastly different directions. Christians, then, who embrace the Bible as God's written revelation, must seek to answer the question of where the Koran came from.

Simplistic Characterizations?

With perhaps more zeal than wisdom, some Christian leaders over the centuries have characterized Muhammad as a demonically-inspired false prophet, a charlatan, a power-hungry political leader, or more recently, a terrorist. The facts of Muhammad's life do not support such simplistic characterizations. All his contemporary witnesses acknowledge him to be a man of integrity and generally high character. Even as the powerful leader of a growing religio-political movement, Muhammad did not take advantage of his position for personal gain. He rarely indulged his appetites (except in sexual matters, where he carried on an excessive number of polygamous relationships), he tended to his own personal needs when he could easily have relied on others, and he remained consistently devout in his own religious customs.

It is true that he engaged in the practice of caravan-raiding, that he wholeheartedly embraced a polygamous lifestyle (even beyond what was allowed for in the Koran), and that he killed men in battle and had some prisoners and enemies executed for refusing to bend to his will, but in these practices he was very much a man of his times. In seventh-century western Arabia, these were common practices. This does not, of course, make them right. But it does help one realize that Muhammad was not riding roughshod over the moral code of his day.

A Spiritual Seeker

As to his religious life, Muhammad in his younger years would rightly be called a seeker. Often withdrawing to the hills in solitary meditation, he seemed cut from a different cloth from his polytheistic peers.

His unyielding commitment to a monolithic monotheism cut across the grain of his day and linked him early on with both Jewish and Christian tribes over against the majority population of pagans. Perhaps Muhammad saw clearly enough through the created order that the worship of idols was futile and demeaning to the true Creator (see in Rom. 1:20–23 Paul's discussion of what the unregenerate mind is capable of discerning about God through the study of nature). He would then naturally incline himself toward that minority (the Arabian Jewish and Christian tribes in his surroundings) whose principal distinction was the worship and proclamation of the one true God of the Book (i.e., the Bible).

We know from stories in the Koran and Hadith literature, as well as from the early Muslim biographies of Muhammad's life, that he had many significant contacts and relationships with Christians, and to a lesser extent with Jews. It is not hard to imagine that much of the content of Muhammad's early theology was inspired by what he directly learned or indirectly overheard from these sources. His misunderstanding of Christian theology may be attributable either to a paucity of orthodox understanding among the Arabian Christians themselves (after all, they were relatively far from any major centers of Christian learning), or to his unwillingness to probe too deeply a faith whose origins he saw as outside the borders of the Arab peoples. Nevertheless, Muhammad's theology always remained staunchly monotheistic, in line to a significant degree with that of pre-Christian revelation.

A Book of Beauty

There is no hiding from the fact that to Muslims the Koran is the paragon of Arabic literature. Nothing is so exquisite and compelling, they say, as the cadence and literary beauty that infuses Koranic Arabic. So lofty is it that it could only have been crafted in heaven. For Arabic-speaking Muslims, this serves as a primary proof of its divine nature and of Muhammad's claim to be the final apostle sent from God with an infallible Word for the human race. Even non-Muslim, native Arabic speakers admit an almost mystical beauty in the Koran's language.

One of my Syrian relatives, who no longer considers herself a religious Muslim, still declares her belief that at least parts of the Koran must have a heavenly origin because of the effect the composition and sound of the text has on the listener/reader. It is difficult to put into words how this aesthetic element of the Koran affects Arabic speakers. But there is no doubt that its language has become the quintessential mark of elegant Arabic and is widely believed to be unmatchable by any human author.

For non-Muslims, of course, this argument is not so compelling. Though beauty is often the handmaiden of truth, we all know of many instances where beauty is used in the service of falsehood. If, as the New Testament says, the father of lies can appear as an angel of light, we must be wary of necessarily associating beauty with truth. There are well-recognized criteria for determining the truth claims of statements. Literary beauty is not one of them.

But is not beauty the work of God? If so, does this not in itself point to heaven as the source of the Koran? Indeed, Christians believe that God is the ultimate source of all good things, including beauty of all sorts. But this does not necessitate God as being the Koran's author. As we have seen already, Satan is able to spin a false web of beauty to entrap the unsuspecting. And indeed, some critics of Islam have contended that Muhammad's inspiration for the Koran must have come from the devil, since it could not have come from God. But Christians are not forced to such a conclusion. Since human beings are created in the image of God, we recognize that all people are endowed with creative abilities. Some, like Michelangelo, Milton, Shakespeare, and Renoir, are acclaimed as aesthetic geniuses. It is entirely possible that Muhammad should be seen in the same way—a man of rare oracular abilities whose religious insights combined with intuitive poetic expression to produce the material we now know as the Koran.

As we will see in the next chapter, Muhammad's recitations were not produced in the order they now occupy in the Islamic holy book, nor are they all there. How did the spoken words of Muhammad find their way into the written form of the Koran? Were they preserved accurately? When did the Koran come into being in the form with which we are familiar today? To those questions we now turn.

CHAPTER
3

And the Word Became ... Paper?

How did Muhammad's revelations move from oral recitations to written text? Muslim tradition holds that Muhammad was functionally illiterate and so could not have written down what was in his mind and heart. This belief is based on one Koranic text alone (7:157–58), which twice speaks of Muhammad as *al-ummi*. This word is often translated "the unlettered one" and is understood to indicate that Muhammad was unable to read or write.

However, the term may just as easily indicate that Muhammad, though literate, was ignorant of Jewish and Christian teaching. The context of the passage implies that Muhammad did not rely on the teachings of the people of the Book (although he believed his revelations to be in concert with the Old and New Testaments) but received his words directly from Allah. If *ummi* derives from the root word *ummiyya*, which means "illiteracy," then one of these two meanings is most likely: Either he was functionally illiterate or religiously illiterate.

But there is a further possibility. *Ummi* may be derived from the root word *umma*, which means "nation" or "community." In this case, the text would mean that Muhammad was the prophet of the nation (of the Arabs) as opposed to a prophet of Jewish lineage. Numerous other passages in the Koran highlight this claim with proud joy. If every nation was sent a prophet over its history, the Arab people were not to be left out. They, too, have a prophet—and not just a "run of the mill" prophet but an apostle, the final apostle through whom God has sent his final, incorruptible Word to the Arabs.

Was Muhammad Really Unable to Read and Write?

How can we decide which meaning is most likely? There are four other places in the Koran where *ummi* is found in its plural form (*ummiyyun*): 2:78; 3:20, 75; 62:2. In each of these cases, it refers to the peoples outside the nation of Israel, who do not have their own Scriptures and are thus incapable of understanding God's revelation to his people. Muhammad is seen as the key representative of the Arab nation, a people who up until his ministry have been without a Scripture. Thus, Muhammad is given the title of "unscriptured prophet" in Sura 7 in order to emphasize that by the kindness of Allah he is bringing fresh revelation in the Arabic tongue for his kinsmen by race. Through him, the Arabs will have their own book, independent of though (presumably) congruent with the Bible.

If this is the originally intended meaning of *al-ummi*, then there is no reason to suppose Muhammad to have been unable to read and write. Further, the fact that he was a successful merchant of international trade would make literacy skills likely if not essential. If such was indeed the case, then it is not far-fetched to conclude that Muhammad may have himself written down some or many of his recitations. However, the traditions make clear that Muhammad never set about the task of collecting all his revelations into one codex or book.

Muslim tradition instead credits the prophet's followers with ultimately saving his words in written form. Indeed, it specifies that the entire contents of the Koran were written down and preserved in discrete units during Muhammad's life but never compiled in one location until after his death. Though this is unlikely in such a strongly oral culture as that of seventh-century Arabia, one cannot doubt that the prophet's words had been faithfully committed to memory by devoted followers. The Hadith of al-Bukhari (5:155) declares that four Muslims had memorized the entirety of Koranic revelations. While this repository of memory sufficed for the moment, events quickly made it necessary for the Koran to be committed to writing for subsequent generations.

Putting Memorized Words into Writing

Soon after Muhammad's death in 632, a handful of Arabian tribes declared their independence from the Islamic community. Abu Bakr, Muhammad's successor, sent an army to subjugate them in what became known as the battle of Yamama. There a significant number of Muhammad's companions who knew large portions of his recitations died in battle. Indeed, one of those killed was Salim, the freed slave of Abu Hudhaifa, whom Muhammad had named as one of the four best reciters of the Koran. Abu Bakr realized that unless the revelations were captured in print in a duly authorized fashion, the words of Muhammad might die out with the demise of that first generation of converts.

As a result, Abu Bakr commissioned Zaid ibn Thabit, one also well-known as having memorized the bulk of the revelations, to collect all the true words of the prophet and gather them into one book. The two principal sources for his project were the parchments (i.e., sayings written down) and the hearts of the companions of Muhammad (i.e., memorized texts). The story, narrated by Zaid himself, is told as follows in al-Bukhari 6:509:

> Abu Bakr As-Siddiq sent for me when the people of Yamama had been killed. (I went to him) and found Umar bin Al-Khattab sitting with him. Abu Bakr then said (to me), "Umar has come to me and said: 'Casualties were heavy among the Qurra' of the Qur'an (i.e., those who knew the Quran by heart) on the day of the Battle of Yamama, and I am afraid that more heavy casualties may take place among the Qurra' on other battlefields, whereby a large part of the Qur'an may be lost. Therefore I suggest, you

(Abu Bakr) order that the Qur'an be collected.' I said to Umar, 'How can you do something which Allah's Apostle did not do?' Umar said, 'By Allah, that is a good project.' Umar kept on urging me to accept his proposal till Allah opened my chest for it and I began to realize the good in the idea which Umar had realized." Then Abu Bakr said (to me), "You are a wise young man and we do not have any suspicion about you, and you used to write the Divine Inspiration for Allah's Apostle. So you should search for the Qur'an and collect it in one book." By Allah, if they had ordered me to shift one of the mountains, it would not have been heavier for me than this ordering me to collect the Qur'an. Then I said to Abu Bakr, "How will you do something which Allah's Apostle did not do?" Abu Bakr replied, "By Allah, it is a good project." Abu Bakr kept on urging me to accept his idea until Allah opened my chest for what He had opened the chests of Abu Bakr and Umar. So I started looking for the Qur'an and collecting it from palm stalks, thin white stones and also from the men who knew it by heart, till I found the last Verse of Surat At-Tauba (Repentance) with Abi Khuzaima Al-Ansari, and I did not find it with anybody other than him. The verse is: "Verily there has come unto you an Apostle from amongst yourselves. It grieves him that you should receive any injury or difficulty ..." (9:128–129). Then the complete manuscripts of the Qur'an remained with Abu Bakr till he died, then with Umar till the end of his life, and then with Hafsa, the daughter of Umar.

Contradicting Popular Muslim Belief

Unwittingly, this tradition contradicts popular Muslim belief that the entirety of the Koran had been unerringly memorized by a number of Muhammad's followers, whose versions all coincided. Zaid records that he searched through many sources and decided the process was complete only after discovering this last verse, which no one knew except for Abi Khuzaima.[1] Additionally, the fact that Zaid had to undertake this search indicates that there was no unanimity among the *qurra* over the complete text of the Koran. Otherwise, all Zaid would have had to do was to record the recitations of one memorizer rather than gather and sift those of many.

Apparently, however, unknown to Caliph Abu Bakr, other early memorizers had also begun compiling their own versions of the "complete" text. As Zaid was editing what would serve as the basis for a standardized text, other compilations based on the stature of various reciters were being championed in different regions of the growing Muslim empire. Curiously, when Zaid's version was finally completed, Abu Bakr did not seek to impose it on the larger community. It was neither recopied nor presented to the growing empire as the correct and standard text. Perhaps that had been his intention, but he died after only two years in power.

His successor, Umar, also kept the text of Zaid under wraps; indeed, it was kept literally under the bed of his daughter Hafsa, one of Muhammad's widows. Umar's caliphate lasted ten years and was marked by the rapid military expansion of Islam and the consequent influx of great wealth to be managed and distributed. Upon Umar's assassination by a Persian slave, Uthman became the third caliph of the empire, and it fell to him to deal with standardizing the Koran.

Variations throughout the Empire and a Uniform Text

This task was of crucial importance because the rapid expansion of the Islamic world was making centralized rule more difficult as increasing sectors of the conquered populations knew little or nothing of the movement's defining beliefs and practices and felt scant allegiance to Muhammad's successors. It was discovered that in the outlying parts of the Muslim empire, the Koran was being communicated and recited in differing ways, depending on which compilation had won local favor. According to Muslim historical sources, four other major recensions of the Koran, each based on the memory of a highly respected member of the *qurra'* residing in a vital city, were gaining popularity in their respective regions: the version of Ubaiy bin K'ab in Damascus, that of Ibn

Mas'ud in Kufa, that of Mikdad bin 'Amr in Hims, and that of al-Ash'ari in Basra.

A military leader by the name of Hudhaifa bin al-Yaman, having spent time in Iraq, returned in alarm to Caliph Uthman in Medina and reported that the Koran was being recited with extensive variations throughout the empire. According to Hadith tradition, he urged Uthman:

> "O chief of the Believers! Save this nation before they differ about the Book (Qur'an) as Jews and the Christians did before." So Uthman sent a message to Hafsa (Umar's daughter, who had the edition of Zaid) saying, "Send us the manuscripts of the Qur'an so that we may compile the Qur'anic materials in perfect copies and return the manuscripts to you." Hafsa sent it to Uthman. Uthman then ordered Zaid bin Thabit, Abdullah bin Az-Zubair, Said bin Al-As and Abdur-Rahman bin Harith bin Hisham to rewrite the manuscripts in perfect copies. Uthman said to the three Quraishi men, "In case you disagree with Zaid bin Thabit on any point in the Qur'an, then write it in the dialect of Quraish, the Qur'an was revealed in their tongue." They did so, and when they had written many copies, Uthman returned the original manuscripts to Hafsa. Uthman sent to every Muslim province one copy of what they had copied, and ordered that all the other Qur'anic materials, whether written in fragmentary manuscripts or whole copies, be burnt. Zaid bin Thabit added, "A verse from Surat Ahzab (Sura 33) was missed by me when we copied the Qur'an and I used to hear Allah's Apostle reciting it. So we searched for it and found it with Khuzaima bin Thabit Al-Ansari. (That verse was): 'Among the Believers are men who have been true in their covenant with Allah.'" (al-Bukhari 6:510)

This tradition indicates that there were significant numbers of whole collections or fragmentary manuscripts of the Koran in existence during the time when Zaid's compilation was kept in private by Abu Bakr and Umar. Anxiety over real differences in the written text led to the authoritarian standardizing decree of Uthman, so as to keep the

Islamic world united under the rule of the caliphate. In other words, the Koran did not exist as an undisputed, uniform text from the beginning but achieved that status only after Uthman's decree was carried out to burn all competing texts and copy instead the newly reformed text of Zaid ibn Thabit.

Even the casually reported fact of Uthman's commissioning three Quraishi men (who spoke the same Arabic dialect as Muhammad) to work with Zaid in recomposing any sections of the Koran that reflected a Medinan rather than a Meccan dialect of Arabic is startling. It acknowledges an implicit understanding by Uthman, Zaid, and others that Zaid's initial work was not perfect but in need of amending! Furthermore, after this revision is complete, Zaid recounts in another Hadith tradition that he subsequently recalled another verse that had never been put in his now revised edition. He turned again to Khuzaima bin Thabit for its correct form and then added it to the revised manuscript (now found in Sura 33:23). This text as a whole then went forward to the Islamic empire as the standard text alone to be copied and used.

Trying to Explain Differences

Muslim apologists sometimes argue at this point that the differences with regard to the Koran around the empire dealt only with variations in how the text was recited, not with differences in the written text itself. However, if the differences were merely a matter of variant pronunciations of an identical text, such a problem would not be solved by sending to all parts of the empire the same written text that they presumably already had. But, these apologists counter, early Arabic was a fully consonantal language. The writing of the Koran was built on the use of early Arabic's seventeen consonantal letters. However, when diacritical points are added, the number of distinct letters increases to twenty-nine.

On top of that, only when further vowel pointings are added to the consonants does one know exactly how the written words are to be pronounced and understood. Perhaps, say the apologists, this is what Zaid's revised edition of the Koran was meant to do—enable Muslims across the expanding empire to know exactly which letters and vowels were intended in the uniform written text that they presumably already had.

But this viewpoint runs counter to the facts. If the issue were simply one of diacritical marks, these could easily have been added or changed without burning the other extant manuscripts. Even more telling, however, is the history of manuscript transmission of the Koran from its earliest days. All of the earliest manuscripts in existence were written with no diacriticals. Indeed, there are no examples of Korans with full pointing until more than two hundred years after the death of Muhammad, or one hundred and eighty some years after Zaid's version

First page of the Koran. Hand-copied in Arabic by Naskhi Ayyub ʾAli Muhammad Rahim al-Nisawi, n.d. *World Treasures of the Library of Congress: Beginnings* Exhibit.

became the standardized text of Islam. Apparently, then, the issue confronting Uthman was not one of variant pronunciations of the same text but of conflicting texts themselves.

Such an admission deals a death blow to the popular Muslim claim that the Koran came straight from the mouth of God to Muhammad and was recorded perfectly and transmitted to the world without error. Since Muhammad's defense of his apostleship rests on the perceived miraculous nature of this book and its divine basis, the evidence presented from sources within unimpeachable Muslim traditions casts grave doubts on Muhammad's claims as well as the Koran's reliability.

There is no doubt that from the time of Uthman's standardization, the Koran has been transmitted for thirteen centuries with remarkable accuracy. This is a testimony to the care and devotion of Muslim scribes and the larger Islamic community, as they handle with utmost attention to detail what they believe to be the unadulterated Word of Allah. But a stream can only be as pure as its original source. If the spring of Zaid's revised Koran is itself compromised and uncertain, the fact that it has been pumped through clean pipes since then does not alter or mitigate its original impurities.

A Matter of Control?

Unfortunately, Uthman's efforts to destroy all rival texts have prevented the fields of literary and historical criticism from creating a trustworthy "critical edition" of the Koran based on a detailed comparison of the earliest competing manuscripts. If Zaid's work had itself been based on a gathering of all these various manuscripts and a reasoned process through a council of Muhammad's companions to hammer out the "best" among variant readings, we might have more confidence in what has come down to us today. But that did not happen. Uthman was not interested in theological integrity but in political unity. Zaid's text became the preferred one, not because it was right where the others were wrong, but because it was the one in Uthman's control and thus could be enforced throughout the empire as the mandated text of the Koran.

Political control was important because Uthman had become an increasingly unpopular leader and his position was precarious. As a result of nepotism, by which he installed his unworthy Umayyad family members into positions of high authority within his caliphate and spurned many longtime associates of the prophet, Uthman never lacked for enemies.

The growing opposition to this caliph, particularly by those with popular religious authority (including the *qurra*', who were the de facto gatekeepers of the revelation of Muhammad), served as a palpable danger to Uthman's perceived legitimacy. By imposing his preferred text on these highly respected religious leaders, he attempted to undermine their support base and thereby remove the threat of their opposition in religious and political matters, since "his" Koran would become the version consulted for all questions of faith and life. Not surprisingly, the opposition seethed with resentment over this, and though Zaid's Koran did become the standard throughout the empire, Uthman did not live long enough to enjoy the unification of Islam under his leadership. During an insurrection, he was assassinated.

Rivals Compete

Though in the end Uthman's strong-arm tactics did lead to the adoption of one text over all rivals, the champions of the other versions did not capitulate quietly. Abdullah Ibn Masud in particular contended with good reason that his codex was most reliable and authoritative. After all, he had been one of Muhammad's closest companions from the early days of the prophet's ministry and was singled out by Muhammad for his memorization skills. Tradition records Ibn Masud's self-assessment as primary among the *qurra*'. In one story, he speaks with appropriate humility:

> Shaqiq bin Salama narrates: Once ʿAbdullah bin Masʾud delivered a sermon before us and said, "By Allah, I learnt over seventy Suras direct from Allah's Apostle. By Allah, the companions of the Prophet came to know that I am one of those who know

Allah's Book best of all of them, yet I am not the best of them." ...
(al-Bukhari 6:522)

But in another account he challenges anyone to equal his memory
regarding Muhammad's revelations:

> By Allah other than Whom none has the right to be worshipped!
> There is no Sura revealed in Allah's Book but I know at what place it
> was revealed; and there is no Verse revealed in Allah's Book but I know
> about whom it was revealed. And if I know that there is somebody
> who knows Allah's Book better than I, and he is at a place that camels
> can reach, I would go to him. (al-Bukhari 6:524)

His stature is supported by the testimony of others (see al-Bukhari
6:522, 525). According to what can be reconstructed from Muslim tradition, there were numerous significant textual differences between the
manuscripts of Zaid and Ibn Masud,[2] not to mention the multiplication of variants found in other major versions being championed in
their respective parts of the Muslim world.[3]

A Mortal Blow at the Foundation?

The existence of such extensive conflicts concerning the actual text
of what purports to be a divine book transmitted to the world free from
error should make all Muslims and inquirers pause. If this evidence,
taken from Muslim sources alone, is accurate (and we have no reason
to doubt it since it comes from believers rather than skeptics), it causes
one to question the foundation of Islam. In fact, since the doctrine of
the infallibility of the Koran is the cornerstone on which Muhammad
and his followers defended his claim to be a true prophet, the unrelia-
bility of the text issuing from the struggle over standardization of core
material from the earliest days after Muhammad's death deals a mortal
blow to Islam's faith claims.

Is All That Allah Revealed Remembered and Recorded?

Beyond this conflict over the actual historical text of Islam, there
is the further issue of whether all that Allah is said to have revealed to

the Arabian prophet was in fact remembered and recorded. Particularly in the early days of the movement, when no one could foresee the role Muhammad's words would ultimately play on the stage of world history, there is question about how attentive he and his early followers were to remember and record his recitations.

To allay the prophet's concern over his own forgetfulness, the Koran relegates the solution to this problem to Allah's sovereignty. Muhammad and his followers will only forget those things that Allah wishes them to lose (86:6–7). Indeed, if Allah causes the people to forget any verse of revelation, he will grant them another that is just as good if not better (2:106). Passages such as these implicitly acknowledge that material from Muhammad's prophetic ministry have been lost or forgotten. One must exercise a leap of faith to believe that nonetheless Allah in some fashion later filled in the gaps, so that all that had been forgotten or incorrectly recalled was perfectly inscribed in the Uthmanic edition of the Koran.

Reading and Understanding the Koran Today

Finally, a word must be said about the various acceptable ways in which the Koran as it stands today may be read and understood in the Arabic language. Uthman indeed standardized the written, consonantal text, but when spoken these consonants must be joined with vowels to form words and sentences. In Muhammad's day, Arabic was written with no diacritical marks; one simply knew from the context which words were appropriate from the meaning of the overall text (the same is true in much Arabic writing today). Often, however, more than one vocalized reading is possible from the same written text. This reality led to some confusion in the early days of Islam over the correct way to recite the Koran. According to one tradition, Umar ibn al-Khattab (who would become the second Muslim caliph) related:

> I heard Hisham ibn Hakim ibn Hizam reciting Surat al-Furqan (Sura 25) differently from me, and it was the Messenger of Allah, may Allah bless him and grant him peace, who had recited it to me. I was about to rush up to him but I granted him

a respite until he had finished his prayer. Then I grabbed him by his cloak and took him to the Messenger of Allah, may Allah bless him and grant him peace, and said, "Messenger of Allah, I heard this man reciting Surat al-Furqan differently from the way you recited it to me." The Messenger of Allah, may Allah bless him and grant him peace, said, "Let him go." Then he said, "Recite, Hisham," and Hisham recited as I had heard him recite. The Messenger of Allah, may Allah bless him and grant him peace, said, "It was sent down like that." Then he said to me, "Recite," and I recited the sura, and he said, "It was sent down like that. This Qur'an was sent down in seven (different) ways, so recite from it whatever is easy for you." (al-Muwatta 15:5)

In another tradition Muhammad declares that it was the angel Gabriel who revealed to him seven equally divinely inspired ways in which the Koran could be read:

Allah's Apostle said, "Gabriel recited the Qur'an to me in one way. Then I requested him to read it in another way, and continued asking him to recite it in other ways, and he recited it in several ways till he ultimately recited it in seven different ways." (al-Bukhari 6:513)

Apparently the reason behind the seven different ways of reading is one of mercy, so that those from dialects other than that of the Qura'ish could find a reading style that better fit their own native speech patterns.[4]

Unfortunately, Muhammad never clarified which seven alternate reading patterns were inspired. After his death, therefore, great latitude was given for differences in recitation, even when there was now one standardized written text. However, in 934, two hundred years after Muhammad's death, a highly regarded Islamic authority with the backing of well-placed jurists determined to bring clarity and finality to this issue. He wrote a book declaring seven of the current readings to be the legitimate ones and all others to be discarded as incorrect. On the force of his personal stature and backing, those seven readings were adopted as the ones delivered by the angel Gabriel, and they are still accepted today. In practice, however, since the time of the printing press, one particular reading has gained ascendancy, and most Korans today contain the Uthmanic consonantal text with diacriticals and vowel pointing known as the Asim or Hafs reading.

Instead of Attacking, Respect and Draw Attention to the Living Word

Muslims are usually so committed to the doctrine of the infallibility of the Koran in both its recording and transmission that the historical evidence briefly related in this chapter will typically have little or no impact on their convictions. While it is important for us to have some knowledge of this field of study so as to be able to respond to the unfounded faith claims of Islam concerning the Koran, we must be careful to avoid showing disrespect to Muslims themselves, who with deep conviction follow the teachings of the Koran out of a heartfelt desire to live lives pleasing to God.

Instead of attacking their cherished convictions, Christians would do much better in conversation with Muslim neighbors or acquaintances to avoid unnecessary controversy by drawing attention instead to Jesus as the living Word of God (a title that, as we will see, even the Koran applies to Jesus). We are not left with dead words on a page to follow slavishly in the hope that we will merit divine attention for our obedience, but God offers us a life-giving relationship with the living Word, who from before all time existed with God and who, according to the Gospel of John, indeed *is* God.

Jesus, this living Word who came to dwell among us, still ministers his grace and truth to all who are hungry to know God. Only he can set free the prisoners—whether those imprisoned by adherence to a written code that brings only death or those imprisoned by a libertine lifestyle of self-gratification and rebellion. He alone is our hope, and the hope of the Muslim—not the Word that became paper, but the One who became flesh and offered himself up in sacrifice for all sinners, who was raised to eternal life, and who even now lives to intercede in love for a wayward world!

Will the Real Jesus Please Stand Up?

Years ago, the television industry featured a program that included a panel of "experts." They were given background information about the unusual career history of a mystery person, say "John Smith," and then were introduced to three contestants who all claimed to be that person. By means of often humorous interrogation, the panelists attempted to discern the truthful contestant from the two impostors. At the end of the segment, the experts each would vote, after which the host of *To Tell the Truth* would ask climactically, "And now, will the real 'John Smith' please stand up?" The goal, of course, was to stump the panel of experts along with thousands of television viewers.

Contradictory Views

Islam claims to offer the world a clear description of the true nature and identity of Jesus of Nazareth. However, this description varies considerably from that of classic Christianity. These two world faiths both claim to be revelation from God. Given that they cannot both be right if they offer contradictory views of Jesus, the average observer is left asking the question: "Will the real Jesus please stand up?"

This chapter will not argue for the historical and theological accuracy of the Bible concerning the true nature and identity of Jesus because many excellent books have successfully undertaken that task. Rather, I will elucidate what the Koran, supplemented by Islamic tradition, teaches concerning Jesus. Since in many places the Koran directly disputes Christian claims about Jesus, we will see clearly the differences between Islam and Christianity.

Many Christians are amazed to discover that the Koran mentions Jesus at all, and even more startled that it has positive things to say about him. Many Muslims are confused by the varied assessments of Jesus they hear from some Christians.

Lunch with Omar

Recently I met Omar at a conference on Christian-Muslim dialogue. Over lunch he told me, "We Muslims have a higher view of Jesus than many Christians I know. We believe Jesus was born of a virgin. Many of my Christian friends don't. We believe Jesus did many amazing miracles, by God's permission; my Christian friends are skeptical. We believe Jesus will return before the end of the world; my Christian friends don't seem to know one way or the other."

It is true that the Islamic picture of Jesus is more lofty than that of theological liberals, who see Jesus primarily as a Jewish itinerant sage who spoke in parables and aphorisms, offering time-bound wisdom that needs to be freed from its cultural chains by enlightened scholars of the West. But this liberal caricature of Jesus is not what the orthodox Christian church has culled from the Scriptures and believed for the last two thousand years. Yet because the church has not spoken clearly and with one voice on the identity of Jesus Christ, Muslims are confused over what we believe and how it relates to what they believe about him.

Moses, Muhammad, and Jesus

The Koran views Jesus as one of the six greatest prophets ever to have lived. According to Muslim tradition, God has sent 124,000 prophets to the people of earth over her history, culminating in the mission of Muhammad. In the Koran, however, only twenty-four are mentioned by name, and of these only Adam, Noah, Abraham, and Moses are accorded the same honor and dignity as Muhammad and Jesus. Moreover, Moses, Muhammad, and Jesus are referred to as "apostles." For Islam this is a technical term indicating an individual to whom the revelation of God's law has been given in book form, which in turn is meant to be taught to the apostle's followers. Thus, Moses was given the *Tawrat* (the Torah), which most Muslims take to mean most of the Old Testament, and this was proclaimed to the Jews. Jesus was given the *Injil* (the Gospel), which is understood as the whole New Testament, and this in turn was proclaimed to the Christians. And Muhammad was given the Koran, which was to be proclaimed first among the Arabs and later to the whole world.

Prophets in the Koran

Moses (*Tawrat* to Jews)		Jesus (*Injil* to Christians)		Muhammad (Koran to Arabs and whole world)	
Adam	Noah	Abraham	Moses	Jesus	Muhammad

Conception and Birth

Jesus' exalted status in Islam is seen not only in his mission as prophet and apostle, but also interestingly enough in the uniqueness of his conception and birth. According to the Koran (3:59), the only figure comparable to Jesus in this regard is Adam, who of course was created with no human parentage. Muslims affirm the virgin birth of Jesus. By a miracle God caused the young virgin Mariam (Arabic for Mary) to conceive without the aid of a man and informed her of the special role her son would play.

It is fascinating to discover, however, that the Koran not only speaks highly of Jesus but also elevates Mary to a position beyond all other women. According to Sura 3:35, Mariam is the offspring of Hannah and Imran and said to be of priestly descent. From the womb the child is dedicated to the special service of God, though apparently Hannah expected God would give her a son. According to 3:36, when Mary was born, Hannah bowed to the will of God, although she could not understand how God would glorify himself through a female. Nonetheless she said, "I have named her Mariam, and I commend her and her offspring to Your protection from the evil one, the rejected."

This account perhaps finds its basis in late patristic theology, where Christian theologians were concerned to protect the doctrine of the sinlessness of Jesus and so began to teach the immaculate conception of Mary—that is, that Mary was free from the touch of the devil so as to be a pure receptacle through whom the Son of God could be brought into the world. Though there is no such teaching about Mary in the Bible, the Koran and Islamic tradition champion this elevated view of Mary's nature. Indeed, one Hadith tradition says, "Every child that is born is touched by Satan and this touch makes them cry, except Miriam and her son" (al-Bukhari 6:71).

Islamic tradition also holds that Mary was raised in the temple under the watchful eye of Zechariah (chosen from among other priests by the casting of lots), who would later become the father of John the Baptist. In 3:37 the Koran asserts that whenever Zechariah pops in to check on her situation, she is always already supplied with ample provision. So he asks her one day, "O Mary! From where does this come to you?" She responds, "From God: for God provides sustenance to whom He pleases, without measure."

Again, there is nothing in the New Testament to support such traditions about Mary. Where might Muhammad have come up with these accounts? Not surprisingly, in Christian apocryphal literature of the centuries preceding Muhammad a number of stories embellish the life of Mary in precisely the way the Koran and later Islamic tradition report (see, for example, the Protoevangelium of James the Less, written centuries before the birth of Muhammad, which contains clear and undeniable parallels to the Koranic account). It is highly likely that Muhammad had heard these stories among the Nestorian Christian tribes of the Arabian peninsula, who had a high view of Mary in her role as childbearer of the Son of God.

Later in Sura 3:45–49 Mary entertains angels, who reveal to her, "God gives you glad tidings of a Word from Him: his name will be Christ Jesus, the son of Mary, held in honor in this world and the hereafter and of [the company of] those nearest to God; he shall speak to the people in the cradle and in maturity. And he shall be [of the company] of the righteous." Mary responds in wonder, "O my Lord! How shall I have a son when no man has touched me?" God apparently responds directly to her (the verb is masculine singular—"he said"), "Even so: God creates what He wills: when He has decreed a plan, He but says to it, 'Be,' and it is!"

Mary or Miriam?

This story of the Annunciation is told later in Sura 19, which appropriately enough is entitled "Miriam." Beginning with verse 16, we read that Mary has withdrawn from her people to an eastern place to be alone. God sends his spirit to her, appearing in the form of a man. In fear, Mary prays for God's protection from this interloper. But the angel responds, "I am only the messenger of your Lord [to announce] to you the gift of a holy son." Mary objects that she has never been touched by a man, but through the angel God declares, "It is easy for me, and we will make him a sign to me and a mercy from us, and it is a matter that is decreed." So Mary miraculously conceives and withdraws from public view.

When the time of birth arrives, she finds herself in extreme pain at the base of a palm tree. Not unlike Job in his anguish, Mary rues the day she was born as the birth pangs increase. Just then a voice calls out from beneath her, "Do not grieve; your Lord has provided a stream below you; and shake toward you the trunk of the palm tree, and it will let fresh, ripe dates fall on you. So eat, drink and refresh yourself."

In due time, Mary brings her newborn son to her people, who remain aware of her unwed state. They rebuke her, "O sister of Aaron, your father was not a bad man and your mother was not a prostitute." Mary refuses to defend herself but points instead to the baby. Understanding her meaning, the people cry out, "How can we speak to one who is a boy in the cradle?" But to everyone's amazement, the baby Jesus speaks:

> "I am indeed God's servant. He has brought me the Book [the Gospel] and made me a prophet. He has made me blessed wherever I am, and has enjoined on me prayer and almsgiving as long as I live. He has made me kind to my mother, and not overbearing or miserable. So peace be upon me the day I was born and the day I die and the day I am raised up alive." (19:16–33)

One of the interesting sidelights of this text is the title "sister of Aaron" given to Mary. Since in Arabic there is no distinction between the names Miriam and Mary, and since Muhammad was not well acquainted with biblical history and chronology, it is likely that he confused Mary the mother of Jesus with Miriam the sister of Moses and Aaron (see Ex. 15:20, where she is specifically referred to as the sister of Aaron). The fact that Muhammad names Imran (Arabic for the Hebrew Amram) the father of Mary underscores the probability of this view, for in Numbers 26:59 we are told that the father of Aaron, Moses, and Miriam was Amram.

Miracles in the Koran

Another fascinating feature of the Koranic account of Jesus' nativity is the extrabiblical miraculous story of his infant preaching. While in Islam all true prophets are to be distinguished by their working of miracles, according to the Koranic record only Jesus is brought into the world by a miracle, only he performs miracles while still in infancy and childhood, and only he is spared death by God's miraculous intervention.

Indeed, Jesus' life and ministry seem especially marked by miracles, in distinct contrast to that of Muhammad. Muslims will point out quickly that the Koran makes clear that Jesus' supernatural works are only possible because of God's permission. Christians certainly would not object to that point, but remain curious why God would do through Jesus such great miracles as are recorded or listed in the Koran, while Muhammad has little or no miraculous ministry. In addition to healing the blind, cleansing lepers, and bringing the dead back to life, Jesus performs two miracles according to the Koran that are not recorded in the New Testament.

(1) In 5:115–18, the disciples ask Jesus to petition God to send down a banquet table from heaven for their nourishment and reassurance that they are on the right track in following Jesus. Jesus asks, God responds. But God also speaks a sober warning to the banqueters: "Verily I am sending it down to you, so whoever of you disbelieves afterwards, I will punish him in a way in which I will not punish anyone else in all the world." Since there are no records in Christian literature (even in apocryphal gospels) of anything approaching a miracle like this, many Christian thinkers suggest that the true source for this story is to be found in the Last Supper, which Jesus ate with his disciples, and its distortion is due to the paramount importance the meal acquired in the subsequent life of the church. Since Muhammad's knowledge of the New Testament was scant, it would not be surprising for him to misunderstand or embellish the traditions surrounding the sacrament of the Lord's Supper.

(2) Both 3:49 and 5:113 refer to another extracanonical miracle that in the Koran becomes a sign to demonstrate Jesus' apostleship to the Jews. God appoints Jesus to this position and gives him a particular message for Israel: "I have come to you with a sign from your Lord, in that I make for you out of clay, as it were, the figure of a bird, and breathe into it, and it becomes a bird by God's leave." Interestingly, both the Infancy Gospel of Thomas and the Protoevangelium of James, composed at the latest in the third century A.D., contain accounts of Jesus as a five-year-old boy shaping twelve sparrows out of mud or clay and then miraculously giving them life. It is reasonable to speculate that Muhammad heard Christians telling these apocryphal stories and incorporated them into his personal portrait of Jesus.

Rejecting Jesus As Divine

Christians, of course, proclaimed that Jesus was God, who had incarnated himself in human flesh. More specifically, they asserted that God was a Trinity of being, who had revealed himself in the three eternal persons—Father, Son, and Holy Spirit—and that it was this second person, the Son, who had taken on human nature and identity in Jesus six hundred years prior to Muhammad's public ministry. How much of this theology Muhammad actually understood is open to question, but it is certain that he rejected the possibility that Jesus could be divine. Not unlike the Judaism of Jesus' day, Islam as taught by Muhammad rejected out of hand the notion that the divine could in any sense be identified with anything in the created order. To claim such would amount to idolatry, and Muhammad placed idolatry at the top of his list of sins.

For Muslims today, this sin, known in Arabic as *shirk*, is still the worst of all sins. *Shirk* literally means "association" and refers to the linking of anything in creation with the eternal God so as to offer it worship. When Christians offer worship to Jesus, Muslims see the sin of *shirk* in action, because in their minds the followers of Christ are deifying one who is only a man and thus raising a rival to the one true God.

So the Koran rails against the Christian preaching of the Trinity, and by way of corollary against the divinity of Jesus Christ. Found particularly in two suras composed toward the end of Muhammad's life at Medina, these prohibitions show a surface familiarity with Christian doctrine but betray a deeper ignorance or misunderstanding of orthodox claims. Sura 4:171 declares:

> Christ Jesus the son of Mary was no more than an apostle of God, and His Word, which He bestowed on Mary, and a Spirit proceeding from Him: so believe in God and His apostles. Say not "Three": desist. For God is one God. Far be it from Him that He should have a son!

Likewise in 5:76, the Koran pronounces this judgment: "They do blaspheme who say, 'God is the third of three in a Trinity,' for there is no god except One God. If they desist not from their word (of blasphemy), truly a grievous penalty will befall the blasphemers among them." Later on in the same chapter, the Koran portrays God as speaking to Jesus concerning this claim to deity (5:119–20):

> And behold! God will say, "O Jesus, son of Mary, did you say to men, 'Take me and my mother as gods besides God?'" He will respond, "Praise be to God! It is not fitting for me to say what is not mine by right. If I had said it, Thou wouldst have known it. Thou knowest what is in my heart, but I do not know what is in Thy heart. For Thou knowest in full all that is hidden. I never said to them anything except that Thou didst command me, 'Worship God, my Lord and your Lord.'"

Three Gods?

Clearly these passages show an understanding that Christians claimed a "threeness" about God and that Jesus was one of the three. But just as clearly we see that Muhammad knew nothing of the orthodox doctrine of the Trinity, comprised of Father, Son, and Holy Spirit. Instead, he pictures the Trinity as a family of three "gods," comprised of the true God, of Mary, and of their offspring Jesus. So in 5:76 the reference is to Jesus as the "third of three," and the particular blasphemy envisioned there is the assertion that Jesus is God. Likewise, 5:119 shows Muhammad's misconception that Christians were claiming that Mary and Jesus were to be worshiped as gods alongside the one true God. Thus the Arabian prophet fails in two ways to grasp the Christian message concerning the Trinitarian nature of God.

(1) He points to the wrong triumvirate of God, Mary, and Jesus, thereby demonstrating a faulty view of a trinity based solely on human familial relationships. He apparently believed that Christians claim that the one true God entered into sexual union with Mary and thus fathered a son named Jesus, whom Christians now wrongly worship as the Son of God.

(2) Muhammad views Christians as tritheists rather than trinitarians. That is, he assumes that Christians really intend to worship three

gods rather than the one God who has revealed himself in three persons, all of whom share the same essence and nature. Granted, the doctrine of the Trinity is not easy concept to grasp, much less to assimilate into one's worldview, but either Muhammad's Christian contemporaries failed to clarify what they meant or Muhammad failed to pay attention to what they said. Either way, the last thirteen hundred years have been ones of continued ignorance and misunderstanding by the Muslim world of Christian theology, because Muslims have been taught that the Koran correctly portrays whatever it speaks about.

The Holy Spirit As Gabriel

Since the Koran never speaks about God as Father, it necessarily refuses to speak of Jesus as his Son. Thus, two of the traditional Trinitarian names are anathema to Muslims. Interestingly, the term "Holy Spirit" is mentioned three times in the Koran (2:87, 253; 16:102); in the first two instances, this is the being who strengthens Jesus for his ministry; in the third, it is the one who brings the message of the Koran to Muhammad. Hence, the general consensus among Muslim scholars is that the Holy Spirit is merely another title for the angel Gabriel, because both the Koran and the Islamic tradition claim Gabriel as the agent of God's revelation to Muhammad. As a result of these "givens" from the Koran, Islamic theology provides scant groundwork for Muslims to understand, much less give credence to, a genuine Christian explanation of the Trinity. Therefore, Jesus is never accorded the title Son of God, much less God the Son, the second person of the divine Trinity.

Son of Mary

Muhammad's strong reaction to Christian claims is shown by his preference for speaking of Jesus as "the son of Mary." By far the most ubiquitous title for Jesus in the Koran, this one seeks to emphasize the limits of Jesus' nature as completely and solely human. This, of course, accords with Muhammad's view that all God's prophets, exalted though they are in his plans and purposes, are nonetheless merely human. So he rails against the scarcest hint of divinity associated with any spiritual leader:

> The Jews say Ezra is the Son of God; and the Christians say that the Messiah is the Son of God; that is what they say with their mouths, imitating the sayings of the unbelievers of old. God fight them! How they lie! They have taken their doctors and monks as lords besides God, and the Messiah, son of Mary, when they were commanded to worship only one God. There is no God but He. Praise and glory to Him! Far be He from what they associate with Him! (9:30–31).

Ironically, however, the title "Son of Mary" has a dissonant ring to it in the Islamic mind, where sons are always known by their relationship to their father. The fact that Jesus is spoken of with relationship to his mother underscores the fact that he has no earthly father and so stands apart from every other man to walk the earth since Adam.

Nevertheless, Muhammad declares Jesus to be simply one from a long line of prophets, who therefore brought no new revelation but only the same message that God had given his prophets in every age and among every people group. Muhammad was convinced that the message of the Koran was nothing new in the history of the world; rather, it was a recapitulation of the revelation given first to Adam and trumpeted in turn by every true prophet down through the centuries. Though this truth could be (and often was) subsequently lost or twisted by human beings after the ministry of a prophet, God promised to send a new prophet to bring light where there was darkness, truth where error had prevailed. For Muhammad, there was no progressive revelation, only the faithful declaration of what God had always made known to human beings: that there is only one God, the Ruler and Judge of all creation, and that human beings owe him their full submission and allegiance.

Thus, the ministry of Jesus was no different from that of any previous or subsequent prophet. Sura 42:11 declares to those under Muhammad's ministry: "He has ordained to you with respect to religion what He enjoined on Noah and what We revealed to you, and what We enjoined on Abraham and Moses and Jesus, namely, 'Establish the religion, and do not divide concerning it.'"

Rejection of Titles Linking Jesus with God

If, then, Jesus' mission reflected the same divine purpose as that of Muhammad (and every other prior prophet), nothing Jesus could have said or done would cause him to be exalted beyond the ranks of mere mortals. Muhammad therefore rejected any titles for Jesus that linked him with activities and honors reserved for God alone. The Koran refuses to describe Jesus in the ways most commonly found in the New Testament, such as Lord, Judge, Savior, and Redeemer.

It is no secret that the earliest rallying cry of the fledgling New Testament church was "Jesus is Lord." For Jews (as all the earliest Christians were) to ascribe this central divine title to Jesus was astonishing, for it flew in the face of their radical monotheism. By calling Jesus "Lord," they demonstrated their conviction that the man Jesus was to be identified with the covenant God of the Old Testament, whose primary title in the Hebrew Scriptures was "Adonai," having been substituted in reading for the Tetragrammaton YHWH (Yahweh) and translated into English as "Lord."

Likewise, in early Christian history one of the functions most commonly ascribed to the risen Lord Jesus was that of "Judge." The last line of the Apostles' Creed that refers to Jesus says, "He will come again to judge the living and the dead." This summarizes the Christian view that at his second coming, Jesus will not only usher in the end of history but also sit on the throne of judgment, in order to determine the final disposition of all things and all people.

Denying the Redeemer

As we have seen, Muhammad could not abide the claims of any human to divinity, so he denies these titles to Jesus and returns their honor and function to Allah. Concerning the gospel proclamation that

Jesus is the world's only Savior and Redeemer, the Arabian prophet also attacks these claims on two fronts. (1) He denies that sin is a deadly enough reality as to place human beings beyond their own rescue. Instead of having a fallen nature bent on disobeying God, people commit sins primarily because of forgetfulness. The solution to this problem is to submit wholeheartedly to Allah and follow the regimen of religious practices that Muhammad prescribes so as always to keep before one's mind the duties and responsibilities of human beings to their Creator, and then to carry out these commands. Thus, there is no need of a Savior because every human being has the opportunity to right his or her own wrongs before Allah, who quickly forgives the past offenses of those who demonstrate the seriousness of their submission.

(2) Muhammad denies that Jesus ever sacrificed himself on the cross for the human race. Islam does not have a sacrificial system as part of its ethos, although strangely the greatest holiday of the Muslim calendar is the *Eid al-Adha* (lit., "the feast of sacrifice"). On the day of sacrifice, Muslims are to ritually slay a large beast (camel, cattle, or sheep) with the emphasis on the spilling of its blood, but they are given no theological reasons why this is important. Many Muslims connect this event with the event in Abraham's life where he demonstrated a willingness to sacrifice his own son in obedience to God, but the Koran offers no clue in this direction. So the holiest holiday in Islam underscores the theme of sacrifice and spilling of blood, but with no significant rationale. The idea of atonement for one's own sins is completely lacking.

It is not surprising, then, that Muhammad rejected the notion of Jesus as the Lamb of God who takes away the sin of the world. To short-circuit this claim among Arab Christians, he declared (with no attempt to marshal any evidence) that Jesus never died on the cross but that God rescued him before death and took him up to heaven. In 4:155–56 we read, "As for their [the Jews] claim, 'Verily we have slain the Messiah, Jesus the son of Mary, an Apostle of God,' yet they slew him not, nor crucified him, but they had only his likeness. . . . They did not really kill him. On the contrary, God raised him to Himself, and God is mighty and wise!" (see also 3:55).

Though Islamic scholarly opinions on what actually happened during the crucifixion vary widely, one of the most common explanations given is that God fooled the Jews by changing the facial features of Judas to look like Jesus; He took Jesus to heaven and allowed the Jews to seize Judas and crucify him, while all the time thinking they were executing Jesus. Thus, in Allah's wisdom, the good prophet Jesus was protected, and the traitor received his just recompense. For Muslims, then, the cross bears no redeeming significance, since Jesus did not die on it, and presumably has not yet died, since God spared him from death by taking him directly to heaven.

Return of Jesus to Earth

What, then, of Jesus now? Though the Koran is silent here, Islamic tradition clearly has the prophet Muhammad claiming that Jesus will return to earth to usher in the end of time. When he comes, it will be as king over all humanity. Under his reign, all will prosper, Islam will extend over all the earth, and evil will wither away. One tradition claims that Jesus will marry and have children, rule for forty-five years, and then die in old age. The place of his burial will be between Abu Bakr and Omar (the two earliest caliphs of Islam) in Medina, and he and Muhammad will rise together in the day of resurrection.

Three Final Titles

The picture that the Koran paints of Jesus is of an exalted spiritual man, called to be one of Allah's most highly honored prophets. Muhammad, as the last of the prophets, retains the highest honor among Muslims, but the Koran recognizes the uniqueness of Jesus' birth, the extent of God's miraculous power coursing through his ministry, the controversy surrounding his death and ascension to heaven, and his role as the harbinger of the end of the age. In these ways, Muhammad as it were plays second fiddle to Jesus. Even though the Prophet seeks to demote

Jesus from the stature he enjoys among Christians, his language and acknowledgments retain vestiges of biblical teaching. Three final titles for Jesus found in the Koran demonstrate this.

(1) *Messiah*. This word is found in the Koran only with reference to Jesus. Muhammad could not have understood the New Testament import of this term; otherwise he never would have used it of Jesus. Later Muslim commentators have argued that Muhammad only meant the term to be understood in the most basic of senses, as one "anointed" by God for ministry. Were this the case, however, we would expect to see this term linked with other prophets mentioned in the Koran, and this is never the case.

(2) *The Spirit from God*. No one else in the Koran, including Muhammad, carries this title (4:169). It is impossible to know exactly what Muhammad intends with this phrase, but certainly by it he emphasizes the closeness of Jesus to Allah. Similar to Hebrew, the Arabic word for "spirit" can also mean "breath." If Jesus is thought of as God's breath, he becomes the animating divine force that brings life into the world (see Gen. 2, where God breathes into Adam's nostril the breath of life, "and Adam became a living being"). Almost certainly Muhammad was not thinking consciously of this, but the fact that he uses such a unique phrase for Jesus indicates that he has been deeply influenced, perhaps in subconscious ways, by Christian theology.

(3) *The Word of God, the Word of Truth*. It is unwarranted to believe that Muhammad ever read the Gospel of John and thus that there is anything of a *logos* Christology behind his use of these terms in 4:169 and 19:35. But it is undeniably fascinating that Muhammad should have used such language of Jesus, particularly in a culture where honor, wisdom, and power were so intimately wedded to the spoken word. To speak of Jesus as "God's Word" is to accord him the highest honor imaginable in seventh-century Arabian culture. As with each of the previous titles, *Word of God/Word of Truth* is unique to Jesus in the Koran. No other human being shares this honor; only Jesus has this stature. But the Koran is a copy of an eternal book in heaven, whereas Jesus epitomizes

the living mind and heart of God. He is the conscious, living agent in and through whom God's Word is manifested to the world.

A Springboard for Sharing?

Many Christians are astounded to discover the amount of truth concerning Jesus found in the Koran. This could be strong grounds for hoping that the Koran itself might serve as an evangelistic springboard for sharing with Muslims more fully the good news of Jesus—except for one fact: The Koran explicitly denies the divinity of Christ along with its corollary doctrine, the Trinity. Since Muslims are repeatedly schooled in the dogma that the Koran contains final truth, they are universally unwilling to look at sources outside the Koran to judge anything written in the Koran.

Many years ago, while living in Arizona, I met a young Muslim grad student at the Thunderbird International School of Business Management. As we struck up a friendship and Hussein discovered that I was a pastor, our conversations often turned to religious questions, and particularly to the question of how to understand Jesus and his mission. Surprised that a Christian had read the Koran and was conversant with Islamic theology, Hussein asked me why I didn't accept its conclusions about Jesus over the Bible's claims. After dealing with the issues of the Bible's accuracy over against that of the Koran, I asked Hussein if he wouldn't agree that the best way to learn about someone you don't have direct access to is to hear what his closest friends have to say about him.

"Well, yes," Hussein conceded, "but in this case, though Muhammad was six centuries removed from Jesus, he was being infallibly directed by Allah's angel of revelation."

"But, if what Jesus' closest friends said about him differs so fundamentally from what Muhammad said, doesn't that raise questions as to the accuracy of Muhammad's recitations regarding Jesus?"

"No," Hussein responded. "It shows the inaccuracy of the reports attributed to the friends of Jesus." I then challenged him to read for himself the Gospel accounts before making up his mind so arbitrarily. Since

I had read the Koran, he felt obliged to concede that he ought to at least read the New Testament. Yet in that year before he returned home to the Middle East, he never seemed to get around to opening the text.

Winning through Love

I share this story only to highlight the immense barriers facing Muslims in hearing the truth of the gospel. Most Muslims have been raised to avoid the Bible as a book corrupted by the agents of Satan and thus permeated with error. The only safe revelation, in their mind, is the Koran. Hence it is extremely difficult to get Muslims to read the Bible or any portion of it. While they may admire a Christian's dedication in reading and knowing his own Scriptures, they are wary of reading it for themselves.

As a result, the closest that many Muslims may get to seeing a true picture of Jesus is what they see in a Christian who befriends them, or even better, a Christian community that opens its arms in love and acceptance toward them. My own experience mirrors that of many missionaries much more experienced in evangelism than I: Muslims are won to the true Christ the same way most other human beings are—not by argument but by love. Seeing Christ alive in a believer is much more compelling than hearing arguments concerning the divinity of Christ or the need for substitutionary atonement.

I am convinced that the Muslim world can be won to the kingdom of God, but only through the love of God. This will happen once the church again discovers in practice her first love. When God's people once again fall in love with Jesus and his breathtaking glory, the Muslim world will sit up and take notice. But we cannot expect Muslims to take their eyes off the limited truth that they do have until we ourselves are captivated by him who is the Way, the Truth, and the Life.

CHAPTER
5

Not All Texts Are Created Equal

Christians believe the Bible to be the inspired Word of God. Muslims believe the Koran to be the inspired Word of God. Nevertheless, for Christians some biblical texts carry more theological weight than others, and some passages possess lyrical beauty and imagery that set them head and shoulders above other passages of the Bible. Karl Barth, for example, claimed that Romans 5 is the single most important chapter in the Bible from a theological point of view. Many Christians hold up Romans 8 as their favorite in terms of its hope-filled content and triumphal declarations. Others single out the Shepherd Psalm (Ps. 23) or Psalm 139 for their beauty and message.

Certainly in the worship history of the church, texts such as the Lord's Prayer, the Aaronic blessing, the Beatitudes, and the prayers of Revelation have played a prominent role. With regard to systematic theology, Genesis 1–3 and Romans 9–11 have touted out for their towering contributions. As to applied (or moral) theology, the Sermon on the Mount (Matt. 5–7) is the sine qua non of Christian ethical teachings. Considering the full landscape of biblical texts, therefore, one quickly sees that not all texts carry the same weight in the life of the Christian or of the church at large.

The same is true for Islam and the Muslim. Our goal in this chapter is to explore the landscape of the Koran and highlight texts that have risen to prominence in Muslim tradition and practice. As we will see, in addition to utilizing the criteria of compelling meaning and poetic beauty, Islam also appeals to stories attributed to Muhammad in the traditions in order to single out the Koranic texts of supreme value for Muslim life.

Unique Features and Structure of the Koran

Before looking at specific texts, however, it is instructive to consider some textual features and structural aids unique to the Koran. As we have seen, the Koran contains 114 suras or chapters. Besides being numbered, each chapter has a title (or more than one) taken from some word or phrase in the text. The traditions state that Muhammad himself gave each sura its title, but this is hardly likely since most of the chapters were not arranged in their final form until after his death, and often these suras in their present form contain a mix of material from different periods of the prophet's revelatory career.

With the exception of Sura 9, every chapter begins with a phrase known as the *bismillah*, which means literally "in the name of Allah," and as a whole reads, "In the name of God, the merciful, the compassionate." These words are repeated many times a day by devout Muslims, for they form the opening words of the first chapter of the Koran and are therefore a necessary part of the five mandatory daily prayers. No one knows for sure why Sura 9 lacks this formulaic introduction, but there is a strong possibility that originally it formed the second half of Sura 8 and somehow at an early stage became detached and established as a chapter of its own. A close look at the end of Sura 8 and the beginning of Sura 9 shows a continued central theme concerning how Muhammad and his followers are to conduct *jihad* against unbelievers and polytheists. The transition from one sura to the next is almost seamless.

Structurally, the Koran employs devotional aids to help the reader attend to the text. Each of the 114 suras is divided into smaller sections called *ruku'ah*, a word derived from the Arabic word for "bowing." At the close of the recitation of each section, Muslims are encouraged to do obeisance with a reverential bow. These sections are marked by the Arabic letter *'ain* in the margin of the text, which is typically paired with numeric designations indicating first the section number in order from the beginning, and second the number of verses in that particular section.

Additionally, the Koran as a whole is divided into thirty parts of roughly equal lengths so as to help the obedient Muslim who wishes to recite the entire Koran during the thirty days of Ramadan. Each of these parts is called a *juz* in Arabic (or *siparah* in Persian). When Muslims recite large portions of text, they typically complete one or more of these larger segments rather than simply reciting individual suras. Older, handwritten manuscripts regularly mark the beginning of a *juz* with some sort of eye-catching medallion. Modern print editions will often indicate the new section by some special embellishment of the text.

For those with significant amounts of free time, the Koran is also divided into seven partitions (called *manzils* in Persian), so that the Koran may be recited fully in one week. Finally, the Koran is also divided into three large blocks so that one may be totally immersed in the whole text over three days. This, however, is the extreme limit—the holy book is never to be read through devotionally in less than this minimum time period.

Divisions in the Koran

114 suras (chapters)	30 *juz* (parts)	7 *manzils* (partitions)	3 blocks
	For 30 days of Ramadan	For recitation in 1 week	For recitation in 3 days

Other markers can be found in the margins of many editions of the Koran, designed to provide direction for the proper cadence in reciting the written text (i.e., when to take a full breath, when to make a slight pause, and so on).

Reading and Reciting the Koran

Much ritual and formality surround even the private reading or recitation of the Koran. The correct washings are to be performed before it is opened, followed by the prayer, "I seek protection from Allah against the cursed Satan." This is followed by the *bismillah*. During public readings especially, various verbal responses are expected at the conclusion of certain suras:

- At the end of the *Fatiha* (Sura 1) and the Cow (Sura 2), the congregants respond with *Amin* (equivalent to the Christian "Amen").
- The conclusion to the sura known as both the Journey by Night and the Tribe of Israel (Sura 17) elicits the refrain *Allahu akbar* ("God is most great!").
- Sura 67 (Dominion) concludes with a challenge to the listener: "Tell me! If your water were to sink away, who then could supply you with flowing water?" And the expected response of the people is, "God brings it to us, and He is Lord of all the worlds!"
- After reciting the Sura of the Resurrection (Sura 75), which ends with the question, "Is He not able to give life to the dead?" the spoken refrain is, "Yes, for He is my Lord most High."

Likewise, particular verses in certain suras anticipate appropriate verbal responses. For example, in Sura 3 (The Family of Imran), after the declaration early in the chapter, "There is no God but He, the Mighty, the Wise," those present are to respond, "I am a witness to this." In addition to such verbal replies, the physical act of prostration is expected after the recitation of fourteen particular verses sprinkled throughout the Koran in which prostration is mentioned as an element of worship. During such prostrations, ritual invocations are uttered.

Mystery Letters

Of the 114 suras, twenty-nine of them after the *bismillah* begin with anywhere from one to five nonrelated letters of the Arabic alphabet. Muslim scholars claim that these mysterious occurrences have profound religious meanings that are known only to God and perhaps to Muhammad. This posture has not, however, stopped the faithful from speculating about their meanings, and numerous imaginative explanations or theories have arisen. Six of these twenty-nine suras begin with Alif, Lam, and Mim (A, L, and M), six others with Ha and Mim (H, M), and five with the combination of Alif, Lam, and Ra (A, L, and R). One well-known chapter, Sura 36, in fact gets its name from the mystery letters with which it begins: Ya-Sin.

The Most Important Chapter

Far and away the most important sura in the life of a practicing Muslim is Sura 1, called appropriately the *Fatiha* ("the opening one"). Other popular titles for this sura give some indication of its content, place, and application among Muslims. For example, its titles "Chapter of Praise" and "The Seven Recitals" highlight the fact that it contains only seven verses, which focus first on the praise of Allah, followed by petition for his clear guidance. According to numerous traditions, Muhammad is said to have called this sura the "exalted reading," classifying it as the greatest chapter in the Koran and dearer to him than all the treasures of the world. Because of its central place in the required five daily prayers, as well as its popular recitation over the sick to bring healing and over the dead as a means of seeking God's final mercy for them, the *Fatiha* has also earned the title *Umm al-Koran* ("Mother of the Koran"). According to Sura 15:87, the *Fatiha* is the most significant chapter in all the Koran: "And we have bestowed on you the seven oft-repeated [verses], and the exalted Koran."

So important is this chapter that tradition recounts Muhammad having received it twice in revelation, once at Mecca and again at Medina. It is unique from the rest of the Koran in being a prayer directly addressed *to* Allah, while the rest of the Koran claims to be Allah's address to Muhammad, to the Muslim community, or to the human race at large. Muhammad allegedly declared that those who fail to recite the *Fatiha* cannot be credited with having observed prayer. This sura's place at the opening of the Koran stands in stark contrast to the general organizational rule of placing suras in order from the longest to the shortest. In this way, the *Fatiha* stands head and shoulders above all other texts:

> In the name of Allah, the most gracious, the most merciful.
> Praise be to God, the Lord of the universe,
> the Compassionate, the Merciful,
> King of the day of judgment.
> You [alone] do we worship, and to You [alone] do we cry for help!
> Guide us on the straight path,
> the path of those to whom You are gracious,
> not of those with whom You are angry, nor of those gone astray.

According to one Hadith tradition recorded by al-Bukhari, Muhammad enjoined his followers to say *Amin* following the recitation of this sura, with the promise that if their amens coincided with that of the angels, all their past sins would be forgiven.

The Chapter of Purity

Next in importance to the *Fatiha* is another short sura, the Chapter of Purity (112):

> Say: He is God, the One and Only;
> God, the Eternal, the Absolute;
> He does not beget, nor is He begotten;
> And there is none like unto Him.

This chapter emphasizes the uniqueness and unity of the nature of God and serves as a polemic against both paganism ("There is none like unto Him") and Christianity ("He does not beget, nor is He begotten"). It is used regularly in anti-Christian Islamic literature and is well-known throughout the Muslim world, a favorite among calligraphers as a means to showcase their talents. Indeed, a beautiful calligraphic rendition of this sura hung framed on the wall of my father's study for years, even though he was by no means any longer a practicing Muslim.

The Hadith traditions record Muhammad's high estimation of this Sura of Purity. He is reputed to have asked his companions whether any of them could recite one-third of the Koran in one night. When they all responded with shock and dismay, he asserted that the recitation of this sura is equivalent to one-third of the whole Koran. On another occasion, upon hearing a follower recite this sura, Muhammad announced that the reciter was assured of his place in paradise.

The Heart of the Koran

A third chapter highly esteemed by Muhammad is Sura 36, Ya-Sin (noted briefly above). The prophet is said to have declared concerning this sura, "Everything has a heart, and the heart of the Koran is the chapter Ya-Sin. Everyone who reads it, for him God will write rewards equal to those garnered for reading the Koran ten times." Not surprisingly, this sura is often found in Muslim prayer booklets or printed by itself for ease of access. As with the Sura of Purity, Ya-Sin's opening verses are often the focus of calligraphers' skills.

Chapter of the Cow

Finally, the Chapter of the Cow (Sura 2), the longest in the Koran, carries great spiritual weight. "Verily, the devil runs away from the house in which the Sura of the Cow is read," says one of the Hadith traditions. This stature is due in large part to the final two verses of the chapter, concerning which Muhammad purportedly said, "If a person recites the last two verses of the *Surat al-Baqarah* ['the Cow'] at night, that will be sufficient for him." They read as follows:

> The Apostle believes in what has been revealed to him from his
>   Lord, as do the men of faith.
> Each one believes in God, His angels, His books, and His apostles.
> "We make no distinction [they say] between one and another of His
>   apostles."
> And they say, "We hear, and we obey: [We seek] Your forgiveness,
>   Our Lord,
> and to You is the end of all journeys." (v. 285)

> On no soul does God place a burden greater than it can bear.
> It gets every good that it earns, and it suffers every ill that it earns.
> [Pray:] "Our Lord! Condemn us not if we forget or fall into error,
>   our Lord!
> Lay not on us a burden like that which You laid on those before us,
>   our Lord!
> Lay not on us a burden greater than we have strength to bear.
> Blot out our sins, and grant us forgiveness. Have mercy on us.
> You are our Protector; give us victory over the disbelievers." (v. 286)

These verses summarize the central message of Islam and lead into a prayer for mercy and forgiveness.

The Throne Verse

Sura 2 also contains the one verse that Muhammad considered superior to every other one in the Koran. Known as "The Throne Verse," it eloquently underscores the sovereignty of God by asserting his rightful ownership and sustenance of everything that exists, and his knowledge of and permission for all that happens or will happen in the creation:

> Allah! There is no god but He, the Everlasting One. Neither slumber nor sleep overtakes Him. To Him belongs whatever is in the heavens and whatever is on the earth. Who can intercede with Him except by His permission? He knows what happens to His creatures in this world, and what will happen to them in the hereafter. And they will never compass anything of His knowledge except that which He wills. His throne extends over the heavens and the earth, and He feels no fatigue in guarding and preserving them. And He is the Most High, the Most Great. (2:255)

Sura of the Light

One other Koranic verse that is cherished particularly by the mystical wing of Islam known as the Sufis is the Sura of the Light 24:35. Written with delicate poetic beauty, it speaks of the luminous glory of God:

> Allah is the light of the heavens and the earth.
> The parable of His light is as if there were a niche
> and within it a lamp;
> the lamp enclosed in glass;
> the glass as it were a brilliant star, lit from a blessed tree,
> an olive, neither of the east nor of the west,
> whose oil is well-nigh luminous,
> though no fire touched it.
> Light upon light! Allah guides to His light whom He wills.
> And Allah sets forth parables for mankind, and God knows all
>   things.

Finding Protection

For those Muslims worried about evil and seeking protection from human or demonic enemies, the last two suras of the Koran (113–14) are memorized and recited as defensive incantations. Both these short chapters implore the protection of Allah from various assaults instigated by the powers of darkness. Particularly in the world of folk Islam these final suras play a large role in the daily ritual attempts to keep a handle on otherwise overwhelming superstitions:

> Say: I seek refuge with the Lord of the dawn,
> from the evil of what He has created,
> and from the evil of darkness as it spreads,
> and from the evil of those who practice witchcraft, who blow on
>   knots,
> and from the evil of the envier when he envies. (Sura 113)

> Say: I seek refuge with the Lord and Cherisher of mankind,
> the King of humanity, the God of mankind—
> from the evil of the whisperer, who withdraws,
> who whispers into the hearts of mankind—
> among jinns and among men. (Sura 114)

While it remains true in Muslim thought that all portions of the Koran are worthy to be memorized and recited, the greatest merit is attached to those suras and verses we have addressed in this chapter. Muslims around the world will be found reading, reciting, and writing them repeatedly as a spiritual exercise, in hopes of earning Allah's eternal favor. After all, they believe the Koran to have come from the mouth of God and believe further that what God loves best is to hear his own words recited by his creation.

This raises the crucial question of the nature of God and his plan for the world. Is Allah, the God of the Koran, the same as the God revealed in the Bible? Are the theologies of Islam and Christianity compatible? To these colossal and complicated issues we turn in the next chapter.

CHAPTER

6

Is Allah a False God?

Imagine six friends sitting together discussing various subjects when the name "Jimmy Magee" comes up. The first person says, "I've heard that name so many times, but I have never actually seen the man. I'm convinced there's no such person—just a dream in someone's imagination."

The second friend responds, "How can you be so sure? Have you searched through every town and city? I've never really met this Jimmy Magee, but I can't say with any certainty that he doesn't exist."

"Ah, Jimmy Magee," says friend number three, "his name stands for what's best in all of us—we're all Jimmy Magee, if we'd just open up our eyes and pay attention."

"No, no," says the fourth, "there *must* be a real person named Jimmy Magee. I've heard of him—a young, strapping lad who stands about six foot four, plays first base for the Atlanta Braves, and loves country music."

"Well, you're right about one thing," says the fifth friend, "there really is a Jimmy Magee, but you've got the details all wrong. People who know him have described him to me, and I've read about his life. He's not American but English, born and raised in Northumbria. He doesn't know the first thing about baseball, but I hear he's crazy about cricket. He's a freeman of Durham, retired from the postal service, and an avid gardener."

"Yes," the final group member declares. "You're describing the real Jimmy Magee somewhat, but he's so much more. I know, because we've been best friends since childhood. We've been through thick and thin together, and we have shared heart, mind, and soul for over forty years. Let me tell you about the real Jimmy Magee . . . !

If we substitute the term "God" for "Jimmy Magee" in the above dialogue and make the other necessary changes, these friends represent (from a Christian point of view) six possible perspectives on the question of the knowledge of God.

- The first, of course, represents the atheist, certain that there is no God and thus no possibility of knowing such a being.
- The second is the agnostic, uncommitted because of uncertainty.
- The third reflects an Eastern monistic worldview as it might be played out in New Age terms. This person denies the possibility of a real relationship with a real God who is other, because in the end there is no difference between the self and anything else. If all is essentially one, then there is no possibility of real relationship, for relationships demand two distinct persons.
- The fourth friend represents one who feels a deep conviction that there must be a God after all, but who is mistaken about the nature of that one true God and so conjures up a divine image that is fatally misleading.
- The fifth contributor represents one who has gathered a good deal of correct information about God from others to whom God has revealed himself in the past. Nevertheless, this individual lacks a personal sense of who God is and of what God is most passionate about, what his priorities are, what he loves, and what he hates. As a result, the description of God this person offers,

while it contains many important kernels of truth, is nonetheless skewed because he has misunderstood or remained ignorant of the central core of God's personal identity.

- The sixth and final group member represents one who has enjoyed a living relationship with God over many years and whose understanding of God is based on what God has said about himself, on what others who have known God have reported, and on what this believer has discovered concerning God through personal experience—walking through life with God at his side. While this friend would never claim to comprehend all there is to know about God, he would nonetheless assert that his knowledge of God represents an accurate depiction of the essence of what human beings can know about God in this life.

The two views that concern us in this chapter are the fifth and sixth. Writing as a Christian, I place the Muslim believer in the fifth category and the Christian believer in the sixth.

Similarities between Muslim and Christian Views of God

It is grossly unfair to state unequivocally that Muslims and Christians believe in different Gods, for much links both theologies, certainly much more than one finds in comparison with Hindu, Buddhist, or even Mormon theologies. Muslims affirm the complete sovereignty of God, revere his majesty above all created things, see his fingerprints on everything he has made, bow before his judgments and decrees, and believe in the final denouement of all history with the divine Judge separating humankind into the eternally blessed and the eternally damned. God has no equals in wisdom, might, and bounty. Indeed, an infinite chasm of glory separates the weight and worth of God from that of any and every created thing. Hence God has no partners, no one with whom he shares his glory. He alone is eternal, having no beginning or end. He has no needs and dwells beyond time and space.

What about the Name Allah?

So far so good. There is much about which Christians and Muslims agree concerning God. Indeed, of the ninety-nine names (qualities) traditionally associated with God in Islam, Christians can embrace at least ninety, probably more. The Arabic word for God, Allah, is used not only by Muslims but also by Arabic-speaking Christians as they refer to the God of the Bible. It is a contraction of the words *al-Ilah*, which translated literally mean "The Deity," and so serves to highlight God's incomparability.

However, while Christians consider "Allah" to be generic for God, most Muslims do not, arguing instead that "Allah" is unique and underived, constituting God's proper name (much as "Yahweh" would be seen by Judaism). Interestingly, "Allah" was used in pre-Islamic Arabia to designate the Creator and supreme Provider among the pantheon of gods and goddesses. Muhammad, however, denounced this view and sought to clear the skies of any god but Allah. His comprehensive monotheism led to a multitude of additional names for Allah (in the form of attributes), which served to replace the roles previously occupied by lesser deities. Nevertheless, these other names are merely attributes or characterizations of God's activities in the world. God's personal name remains, for all time, Allah.

What the Koran Mirrors of Biblical Teaching

The Koran mirrors biblical revelation in its teachings on God's creation of Adam and Eve, his choice of Abraham as the blessed patriarch, his raising up great prophets like Moses and David for the Israelites, and his detailed laws by which the chosen people were to live. The God of the Bible and of the Koran share much in common, not least because Muhammad derived much of the details of his understanding of God both from conversations with Jewish and Christian acquaintances or relatives and from canonical and extracanonical Judeo-Christian traditions circulating in seventh-century western Arabia.

Differences between Muslim and Christian Views of God

Nevertheless, we must hasten to note many significant differences between Christian and Muslim portraits of God. The first centers on the question of whether God is truly knowable. Islam contends he is not. Indeed, the Koran is not a book of revelation about God himself but of revelation concerning God's will for human behavior and his plan for the created order. Although the Koran declares that all the most beautiful names belong to Allah (7:180) and that Muslims are to use them in calling on him, these names do not describe God's essence but only certain of his activities. In his essence, God is unknowable. One humorous tradition claims that there are really one hundred names for Allah, but only ninety-nine are known to man. The hundredth is known only to God and to the camel, which accounts for its arrogant and dismissive stare.

Muslim philosophers typically employ a theology of negation (defining God in terms of what he is not) in their attempts to describe God. Since God is utterly transcendent, the use of human constructs and creation metaphors to describe God are inadequate and misleading. Yes, Muslims will say, God is most merciful, but his mercy is not what we conceive mercy to be on the human plane. In the end, therefore, such a theology attempts to define God by saying what he is not rather than what he is. We can know details of how God has acted in the past, but we cannot know what really makes him tick. His essence always eludes us, for his nature is beyond our grasp.

The Christian faith agrees that God is too big to be fully comprehended by finite, human minds. Yet it radically disagrees with the assertion that God is unknowable. Our ability to know God depends on two contingent realities: the gracious condescension of God to reveal himself in ways we can rightly understand, and the appropriate receptivity of the human soul to these revelations of God. According to the Christian faith, both of these realities are dependent on the grace of God, which he has exercised most fully through the incarnational ministry of his Son.

The question of God's willingness to make himself known to the human race has been forever answered in the advent of Jesus to this world. He who is the fullness of God dwelling bodily (Col. 2:9) has come to make God known to the world (John 1:18). While we cannot know everything about God, we can know what he chooses to reveal about himself, and according to Jesus he has revealed to us his heart—that he is love and that he seeks to share himself for eternity with us. This love he has demonstrated not only in words but in the flesh, as it were.

Obedience or Relationship?

Here one of the great differences between Islam and Christianity becomes unequivocally clear. In Islam God reveals not himself but his will for humanity. His concern is not to invite human beings into a life-transforming love relationship with himself but to demand rightful obedience to his commands. Under Islam the best human beings can hope for is to be recognized and rewarded as faithful servants. To this end God has sent 124,000 prophets (according to Hadith traditions) down through the ages with the same essential message: "Surrender your lives to the will of God as made known through his various spokesmen." It is our responsibility to obey, and it is on our obedience or disobedience that our final destiny will rest.

In Christianity, by contrast, God is interested not in obedience per se but in the perfection of human life through transformation by the indwelling Spirit of God. This occurs as we live in the presence of God, who has been made accessible to us by Jesus Christ. Through the life, death, and resurrection of the Son of God, we are invited to participate in his relationship with the Father and so are accepted into the family of God, not as servants on the periphery of the estate but as beloved children welcomed into the innermost parts of God's home. The incredible intent of God to open his heart to the human race through the incarnation of his Son sets apart the joy-filled gospel of Jesus Christ from the austere message of Muhammad.

The Solitary Personality of God

The Koran's most dominant declaration about God concerns his unitary nature. Known as the doctrine of *tawhid*, this viewpoint emphasizes the solitary personality of God and guards his essential nature from confusion, mixture, or rivalry with anything in the creation. "Verily, your God is indeed One: Lord of the heavens and of the earth, and all that is between them, and the Lord of every point of the sun's risings" (37:4–5; see also 2:163; 6:19; 16:22; 112:1–4). Those who transgress this most basic truth are guilty, as we noted earlier, of the sin of *shirk* (associating something of the creation with the Creator, attributing divinity to that which rightly finds its place under the throne of God).

In part, this strong emphasis on the divide between God and his creation predisposes Muslims to see God as remote and personally inaccessible. Not surprisingly, the divine attribute most keenly affirmed by Muslims is that of God's matchless power wielded with absolute authority. Little is said in the Koran of God's love, for God is not by nature love. A solitary being cannot be defined as love, nor can such a being exercise love until there is an object to love. Before the creation, God as understood by Islam existed for eternity in his aloneness, stark in his majestic oneness. Even after the creation, Allah is not characterized by the Koran as loving, *except* toward those who have faithfully served him.

This divine love is simply the reward of God's favor on his obedient slaves, not the personal involvement of God intertwining his heart and soul, as it were, with his people. To the Muslim mind, such a divine condescension would signal a weakness in God rather than a strength, for it implies that God is looking for something in others that he lacks in himself. But since God is he whom all others need but who himself needs no one and no thing, this cannot be.

Therefore, Muhammad in the Koran urges his followers, "If you love Allah, then follow me; Allah will love you and forgive you your sins. And Allah is oft-forgiving, most merciful" (3:31). Again in the next verse he proclaims, "Obey Allah and his apostle." Then a final warning is given: "But if they turn back, God loves not those who reject faith" (3:32).

Human love for God is clearly enjoined in the Koran, but as in the case of God's love for human beings, the barrier of divine transcendence proves too forbidding for Muslims to express a heartfelt warmth and intimacy toward God. Love for God shows itself instead as veneration, adoration from afar combined with gratitude for a sovereign's kindness toward those predestined for paradise.

Allah's Will and Fatalism

In the Koran, the transcendent power of Allah is evidenced most comprehensively in his predestining decrees, which determine the course of all that occurs in creation from beginning to end. Everything has been ordered by God's will, and nothing can alter or withstand his determinations. "Allah does what He wills" (14:27); "to Allah belongs the dominion of the heavens and the earth and all that is between them. He creates what he wills. And God has power over all things" (5:17); "all things have been created with pre-ordained decree [*qadar*]" (54:49).

Such a view leads to the fatalistic attitude so prevalent in Muslim lands, where resignation to the vagaries of life and death leads so often to a passiveness in the face of tragedy. A shrug of the shoulders and repetition of the phrase, "What can one do?" is the common response to personal calamity. Even the time of one's own death has already been decreed and cannot be changed, so why struggle? The Koran declares, "No person can ever die except by Allah's leave and at the appointed term" (3:145). Likewise the heart's submission to God is dependent on God's eternal decree; though he sends messengers to speak in the language of their native culture so as to make the divine message clear, nevertheless the listener's capacity to respond rests on God's inscrutable will: "Allah misleads whom He wills and guides whom He wills" (14:4).

Nowhere in the Koran is there a hint that God acts out of love or personal care for those whom he elects, for again this would appear as a divine weakness. One astonishing saying in the Hadith literature sums up this perspective:

> When God resolved to create the human race, he took into his hand a mass of earth, the same whence all mankind was formed, and in which they after a manner pre-existed; and having divided

the clod into two equal portions, He threw one half into hell, saying, "These to eternal fire, and I care not," and projected the other half into heaven, adding, "And these to Paradise, I care not." (Kisasul-Anbiya 21; see also Abu-Dawood 2203; Al-Timidhi 38; Mishkat al-Misabih 3.112–13)

Since the all-powerful Allah needs nothing outside himself, he loves nothing outside himself. Ultimate transcendence prohibits relational nearness. Allah stands above and beyond, ordaining and decreeing all that happens according to his inscrutable, perhaps capricious, will.

What a far cry from God as depicted in the Bible! Certainly sovereign and clearly predestining his elect to salvation, God exercises his will out of a heart of love. He reveals himself as the Lover of his people, who pursues them for their good despite their continued unfaithfulnesses. He is their Good Shepherd, who lays down his life for the sheep of his pasture. He is their Father, who runs to embrace his prodigal son. He is their Savior, who gives up his life as a ransom for many. What Islam decries as shame, the gospel trumpets as glory.

The sacrifice of God, who out of deepest love predestines his Son to the cross so as to reconcile his children to himself, is hardly a sign of weakness. Instead, as the apostle Paul exults, "it is the power of God for the salvation of everyone who believes" (Rom. 1:16). Divine love expresses itself most powerfully through the vast extent to which it is willing to give itself away to others, even to the point of taking on human nature so as to die for human sinners.

Power or Love?

Here we discover another key theological dispute between Islam and Christianity. Whereas for Muslims the primary currency of the divine economy is sovereign power, for Christians it is sacrificial love. Islam commands, "Bow before him"; Christianity invites, "Run into his outstretched arms." These disparate views stem ultimately from the key question of God's nature: Whereas Islam proclaims God as a simple, monistic unity and so refrains from speaking of him as love, Christianity claims that God has revealed himself as Trinity (three eternally existent, coequal persons comprising one essence), whose heart is love.

The Trinity is not three gods but one God, who exists as an eternal community and whose nature is inexhaustible love. He is one being of complex unity, exhibiting a oneness rich with relational diversity. This is why the apostle John in 1 John 4:16 can say, "God is love," for even before any creation, when God existed in solitude, he nevertheless existed in relationship. From eternity, love has characterized the interrelationships among the members of the Trinity. God the Father, God the Son, and God the Holy Spirit define the essence of love in their passionate unity.

Because God is love by nature, when he brought creation into being, it was out of the fullness of his love, with the goal of sharing the overflow of his joy in himself by loving the created order and directing it to find its fullness in his love as well. Especially he set his love on the apple of his eye, those whom he created in his own image (i.e., those capable of covenantal love commitments). Even though as a race we rebelled against this divine love and alienated ourselves from God, he has shown the full extent of his love by leaving his sovereign throne in the person of the Son, stripping himself of divine glory to be born into this world as a human being, living in our midst to make God immanent and accessible, and then voluntarily surrendering his life in a brutal execution so as to satisfy the justice of God against sinners.

In this way God so loved the world, says John, that he sent his only Son to die so that all who give him their allegiance may live (John 3:16). Or in the words of Paul, "God demonstrates his own love for us in this: While we were still sinners, Christ died for us" (Rom. 5:8).

God's Decretive Will

As we have already seen, Islam rejects the incarnation and atonement of Jesus, since the Koran eschews the notion of God as Trinity and specifically of Jesus as God the Son. God remains essentially unknowable and personally unapproachable. His decretive will stands as the focus of the Muslim life, and the believer's ever-elusive hope is that by sufficient obedience he may gain God's eternal favor.

The Christian also takes the decretive will of God seriously, perhaps more so than the Muslim. For the Bible declares that God's law demands full righteousness from fallen human beings, a standard impossible for sinful mortals to achieve (Rom. 3:23). The unrelenting holiness of God requires either our sinless obedience or our punishment. Since the former is beyond us, the latter is our fate. For Christians, the moral demands of God's law would lead to despair if we were left merely to our own resources and the declarations of the prophets. The law can tell us how to behave, but it cannot rescue and empower us. The prophets are good as far as they go, but in the end they stand together with us on this side of the chasm of sin between us and God, and they point beyond the condemnation of the law to the solution for our despair.

That solution materializes in the form of One who has come from the divine side of the chasm, building a bridge across it by his own righteous sacrifice and leading us back with him into the welcoming embrace of his Father and, as a result, our Father too. The prophets, as wonderful as they may be, pale into insignificance compared to the matchless Son of God, who not only declares God's righteous will but fulfills its demands for helpless sinners by bearing our punishment in his body. By this action, received by us in faith, we are justified in God's sight.

Jesus Christ is the love of God incarnate. He is our window into the divine heart of mercy. He is our doorway into the divine embrace of joy. He is the final revelation of God to the world, for he is God himself clothed in our nature so as to make God fully accessible to us. No one before or since Christ has revealed God to the world with such fullness— not even Muhammad—for no one else bears his nature or his mission. That is why the author of Hebrews opens his letter with these words:

> In the past God spoke to our forefathers through the prophets at many times and in various ways, but in these last days he has spoken to us by his Son, whom he appointed heir of all

things, and through whom he made the universe. The Son is the radiance of God's glory and the exact representation of his being, sustaining all things by his powerful word. (Heb. 1:1–3a)

Ignorant of Deepest Truths?

That is why in the final analysis the gospel demonstrates that the Muslim view of God is defective—not completely wrong but ignorant of some of the deepest truths concerning the nature and work of God and therefore unable to lead Muslims into the presence of the God of love, who rescues sinners through Christ.

THE BIBLE	THE KORAN
• God is knowable through Christ.	• God's essence is not knowable.
• God reveals himself.	• God reveals his will for humans.
• God invites life-transforming relationship.	• God demands rightful obedience to commands.
• God is triune.	• God is solitary personality.
• The Bible emphasizes sacrificial love.	• The Koran emphasizes sovereign power.

For all these reasons, I believe on the basis of two biblical passages that Muslims fall into the category of those worshiping the true God in ignorance rather than those pursuing a false god. (1) In John 4:1–26, Jesus initiates a conversation with a woman from Samaria. History records that there was no love lost between Jews and Samaritans. Jews considered Samaritans to be half-breeds because in previous centuries they had mingled Jewish blood lines with those of Gentiles through intermarriage. Furthermore, they accepted only the first five books of the Torah as inspired Scripture, spurning the historical and prophetic books of the chosen people. To top it off, they constructed their own temple in competition with the Jewish temple in Jerusalem.

It would have been easy for the Jews to consider the Samaritans as followers of a false god. During Jesus' conversation with the Samaritan woman, she asks him whether Jews or Samaritans were worshiping in the proper temple. Here would have been a perfect opportunity for Jesus to state clearly that Samaritans followed a false god, but he refuses to do this. He does declare that greater divine revelation has been given to the Jews and that they worship God with greater knowledge, but the Samaritans worship that same God in ignorance: "You Samaritans worship what you do not know; we worship what we know, for salvation is from the Jews" (John 4:22).

(2) Even more telling is what Paul has to say about his fellow Jews who have heard the gospel and rejected it. These are individuals who have rejected Christ as the Son of God and their Messiah, and who see obedience to the law as their means to righteousness before God. Their view of the nature of God accords closely with that of Muslims today. As Paul contemplates their situation, he does not accuse them of turning to a false god but rather of pursuing the true God in ignorance. He writes in Romans 10:1–3:

> Brothers, my heart's desire and prayer to God for the Israelites is that they may be saved. For I can testify about them that they are zealous for God, but their zeal is not based on knowledge. Since they did not know the righteousness that comes from God and sought to establish their own, they did not submit to God's righteousness.

If Paul can say this about monotheistic, non-Trinitarian, Christ-rejecting Jews in his day, it does not seem a great stretch to argue that we ought to be able to say the same thing today about Muslims.

Confrontation or Sharing in Love?

Such an approach toward Muslims would move Christians away from a confrontational agenda to one of positive sharing in the context of love, helping Muslims to discover that they do not have to settle simply for knowing *about* God but that they can now *know* God personally in and through Jesus Christ. They can find for themselves the fulfillment to that deepest longing of every human heart, to learn that they are loved and cherished by God and that they are invited to enjoy his paternal care.

Years ago an aristocratic Pakistani Muslim woman named Bilqis Sheikh made this discovery for herself and recorded her experience in a book with the telling title, *I Dared to Call Him Father.*[1] During her search for God's reality in her life, she turned to a missionary's wife to help her interpret a dream she had had. In the course of their conversation, she asked the woman, "Mrs. Mitchell, do you know anything about God?"

The American woman replied, "I'm afraid I don't know too much about God, but I do know him."

Bilqis Sheikh records her own reaction: "What an extraordinary statement! How could a person presume to know God?" Later in the conversation she ventures further: "'Mrs. Mitchell,' I said, my throat tight, 'forget that I am a Muslim. Just tell me: What did you mean when you said you know God?' 'I know Jesus,' Mrs. Mitchell said, and I know she thought she was answering my question."[2]

Indeed, Jesus is the key to knowing God, for Muslims as for all peoples everywhere. Apart from him, Muslims will continue to practice their faith in ignorance of the great saving truths of the gospel. The church must wake up to its responsibility and privilege as bearer of the good news. As Christians in the first century proclaimed with passion the gospel among the Jews (as well as Gentiles), we Christians in the twenty-first century are called to proclaim with passion and faithfulness this same good news to the house of Islam, so that our Muslim friends may no longer worship in ignorance but discover the divine gift of salvation and love available to them in Jesus Christ.

Streams in the Desert: Jewish and Christian Sources in the Koran

Mighty rivers are formed by the confluence of many sources of water: lakes, springs, run-off, tributaries. The great Mississippi, for example, collects water from as far west as the Continental Divide near the Rockies and as far east as the Eastern Seaboard states. It is the beneficiary of many potent contributors. Likewise, the Jordan River of the Holy Land forms in the Golan Heights at the confluence of three major headwaters (one of these, the Banyas River, is where my father played as a child in the 1930s).

Books are in this sense like mighty rivers. What flows between the banks of the front and back covers comprises the combined input of many streams of information commingling in the mind of the author. Part of the art of literary criticism is the study of written words with a view to understanding the various sources that have contributed to the final product, in the hopes that such analysis will clarify even further the intent of an author or redactor of a written work.

Such studies have been carried out for over two centuries on the Bible, with sometimes helpful insights. Jews and Christians recognize that the inspiration of the biblical text is not negatively affected by the study of extrabiblical sources that may have helped shape its form and content. The inspiration of the Holy Spirit comes not through simple dictation of words directly to scribes but through the complex choreography of events, personalities, divine actions, and human responses so as to clothe heavenly truth in the recognizable garb of earthly realities.

Muslims, however, have a different view of divine inspiration, subscribing, as we have seen, to a dictation theory of revelation. This means, among other things, that Muslims dogmatically reject the notion that Muhammad drew on any earthly sources in the creation of the Koran. They are adamant, even aggressive, in affirming that the Koran came directly from heaven through the mediation of the angel Gabriel and that its thoughts and words are completely and solely the thoughts and words of Allah. To suggest anything less than this is to be guilty of demeaning the Koran, a crime of blasphemy punishable by death in certain Muslim societies (whether enforced by the government or by zealots).

What's the Goal of This Chapter?

The goal of this chapter, therefore, is one that Muslims will find unpalatable. But those not constrained by the religious strictures of Islam are free to utilize the tools of history and reason in seeking to better understand how at least some of the content of the Koran came to be what it is today. Our purpose here is *not* to offend Muslims but to test the claims of Islam as to the divine origins and perfect nature of its central text.

Widely recognized by Western scholars of the ancient Near East is the fact that the Koran contains many traditions and stories found in the world of pre-Islamic Bedouin Arabia, as well as significant portions of material from the Old Testament, from Jewish folklore, and from Christian apocryphal texts. Among such pre-Islamic influences in the Koran are the following:

- commands enshrining the rituals of the annual pilgrimage to Mecca, complete with its originally pagan practices that Muhammad partially reinterprets to fit his novel teachings
- acceptance of the reality of the *jinn*, those mischievous spirits both feared and honored by superstitious Arabians

- focus on a lunar calendar, arising from the powerful cult of a moon god prevalent among the people of the western peninsula.

Our focus in this chapter, however, will be on Jewish and Christian sources that helped shape Muhammad's thoughts and his Koranic recitations. Before we undertake this, though, it is worth emphasizing again that Muhammad was not just a child of his cultural and religious environment. Part of his genius is seen in how he took various traditions and shaped them skillfully for his purposes and how with deep convictions he utilized certain foreign traditions to outlaw or overcome a variety of nefarious tribal practices of his day, such as female infanticide or the treatment of women as mere chattel.

Parallels between Biblical and Islamic Prophets

All students of Islam acknowledge that Muhammad had access to Jews and Christians, with whom he could regularly interact, ask questions, hear accounts of their sacred stories, and receive the seeds for fresh ideas to incorporate into his fledgling Arabian brand of monotheism. His belief that he stood at the end of a long line of prophets (beginning with Adam), bearing the same essential message as they had, meant that he had to see himself in concert with the prophets mentioned in the biblical record, as well as with some named only in local Arabian tradition.

The Koran lists twenty-eight prophets by name, twenty-five of whom by most accounts are recognized as biblical figures (though not all these are called prophets in the Bible). Some of the ways Muhammad describes these seers make it clear that he had no direct access to the Bible himself, but he nonetheless felt it critical to align himself with them. In the process, he assumed that they spoke the same message in their day as he now proclaimed to his listeners, and that the obstacles he faced were the same kind as the opposition they had encountered in their callings.

While Muhammad shows some knowledge (imperfect though it often is) of various biblical figures, he is silent and presumably ignorant about vast sections of the Bible and biblical history. Nothing is mentioned of the major or minor prophets from the eighth century B.C. onward, except Jonah, and most of the Old Testament history of Israel goes unreported except for the events surrounding the Exodus. If we had to rely on the Koran as a source to reconstruct the Bible, we would be bereft of most of the events and teachings it reveals.

According to Islamic tradition, of all the 124,000 prophets sent into the world, only eight received "books" or "pamphlets" to share with their people. These books are 124 in number, with ten having been entrusted to Adam, fifty to Seth, thirty to Enoch (known as Idris in the Koran), ten to Abraham, one to Moses (the *Tawrat* [Torah]), one to Jesus (the *Injil* [the Gospel = the New Testament]), and one to Muhammad (the Koran). Unfortunately, the first one hundred have been lost to humankind, and the two other than the Koran that remain have been tainted by falsehood, so that all that can be trusted now is the Koran. For Muslims, the loss of the former revelations is unimportant, for the essence of these inspired writings has been reproduced fully and purely in the book revealed through the Arabian prophet.

Of the prophets named in the Koran, few get any extended attention. Regardless of their time and place in history, they are portrayed as preaching the same message as Muhammad, with phrasing that often matches Muhammad's own phrasing in other parts of the Koran. To Muslims this makes sense, of course, because these prophets were not delivering their own words but the unchanging words of Allah. To the unconvinced, however, it sounds as if Muhammad is simply exploiting the names and reputations of recognized prophets by putting his words in their mouths in order to bolster his own standing and that of his message. In the main, he shows little significant knowledge of the actual lives and times of most of these prophets.

Extrabiblical Prophets in the Koran

The three extrabiblical prophets mentioned in the Koran are Luqman, Dhuʾl-Kifl, and Dhuʾl-Qarnain. (1) The first is also known as

Luqman the Philosopher and appears in the Koran only in Sura 31, which bears his name as its title. In verse 12 Allah commands Luqman, "Give thanks to Allah," after bestowing on him the gift of wisdom. In verses 13–19, Luqman advises his son, "Do not join others with Allah in worship. Verily, joining others with Allah in worship is a great wrong." He proceeds to warn his son about Allah's omniscient nature from which no deed can be hidden, about the need for strict performance of the ritual prayers, about belief in the one true God and opposition to polytheism, and about the dangers of arrogance.

(2) Dhuʾl-Kifl receives passing attention in Sura 21:85–86 in the midst of a long list of prophets, where he is linked with Ishmael (Ismail) and Enoch (Idris) as belonging to the ranks of the patient and to those receiving God's mercy because of their righteousness. Some commentators identify this prophet as Obadiah or Isaiah, but no evidence supports such a contention. The Koran provides no further material on Dhuʾl-Kifl.

(3) Likewise, the name of Dhuʾl-Qarnain appears only once, in Sura 18:83–98, apparently in response to questions from Muhammad's followers about this mysterious figure. In this section, Allah claims to have established this man in such power that his kingdom stretched from horizon to horizon. One day, Dhuʾl-Qarnain set out on a journey until he found out the setting place of the sun, which according to the Koran was in "a spring of black, muddy water." Near it he discovered a race of people. Allah said to the prophet, "Either punish them or treat them kindly"; in other words, their fate was left up to him. Dhuʾl-Qarnain decided that those who remained polytheists would be punished, but the monotheists who lived righteously would be welcomed into Paradise and receive instruction by him.

Then Dhuʾl-Qarnain heads east until he finds the place of the rising sun and meets a people with no shelter from its intensity. He travels further in a new direction until he discovers two mountains with an intervening valley inhabited by a helpless (or ignorant) people. They cry to him for help: "O Dhuʾl-Qarnain! Verily Yaʾjuj [Gog] and Maʾjuj

[Magog] are doing great mischief in the land. Shall we then pay you a tribute in order that you might erect a barrier between us and them?" (18:94). The prophet rejects their offer of payment but commands them to bring blocks of iron and melt them so as to fill up the pass between both mountains leading into the valley. He then has the people pour molten copper over the iron barrier, as a result of which it becomes impenetrable to Gog and Magog. Dhu'l-Qarnain prophesies that the wall will remain until "the promise of my Lord comes," at which time it will be leveled and Gog and Magog will appear from behind it to face final judgment with all other creatures before Allah.

No one is sure what historical personage Dhu'l-Qarnain is supposed to represent, but his name in Arabic literally means "lord of the two horns," and many Muslims as well as western scholars hypothesize that Muhammad was speaking of Alexander the Great, believing that the title of "two horns" indicates in a poetic manner the extent of his kingdom reaching the known world from west to east. Moreover, some Muslim traditions give Dhu'l-Qarnain the added name Sakandar (an Arabic derivative of the Greek name Alexander) and identify him as king of Greece and Persia. This early linkage, however, proves an embarrassment to later Muslim scholarship, for Alexander was a pagan polytheist, and it would not do to canonize a heathen king as a true prophet of Allah. Unfortunately, no alternate theories carry the support of Islamic tradition.

Biblical Prophets Mentioned in the Koran

Turning now to the biblical characters mentioned in the Koran, we discover that the majority of them also receive limited attention from Muhammad.

Adam and His Unnamed Wife

Stories concerning Adam are found in two suras (2:28–37; 7:10–17). In Sura 2, Allah tells the angels of his intent to create Adam and make him ruler over the earth in his name. The angels question God's wisdom in this, arguing that they would do a much better job of glorifying God in such a task than a corruptible man could. But Allah replies, "I know what you know not." He proceeds to create Adam, teaches him the names of every living thing, then shows his angels all created things and commands *them* to name all that they see. They confess their inability, after which Allah orders Adam to recite all the names. When Adam finishes this task, Allah rebukes the angels for challenging his wisdom in appointing Adam as his vicegerent on earth. He commands the angels to bow before Adam, and all comply except Iblis (Satan) in his arrogance.

God then places Adam and his wife (unnamed in the Koran) in Paradise and directs them to eat with pleasure and delight whatever they fancy with the exception of one tree (whose properties are never described in the text): "but come not near this tree or you both will be of the wrong-doers" (2:35). However, Satan makes them slip up (that is, Adam and his wife disobey God, though we are not told specifically how), and they are punished by being cast down (to earth?), doomed to broken relationships and limited life span. Allah then apparently teaches Adam a prayer of repentance, and after he recites it he receives divine pardon. The story concludes with words spoken by Allah that conveniently echo Muhammad's own message: Whoever follows Allah's guidance will be blessed; whoever disbelieves is destined for eternal fire.

Clearly, the biblical creation accounts of Genesis 1–3 and subsequent Jewish tradition provide the primary source material for the Koran's teaching on Adam. The notion of Satan's rebellion against the honor accorded Adam is a standard teaching in ancient Jewish commentaries, though not found in the biblical text. The idea of a garden paradise, of the freedom to enjoy it except for one tree, and the temptation and judgment are, of course, all found in Genesis 2–3, with much greater detail to supplement the gaps or leaps in the Koranic material.

But there are also some significant differences. In the biblical account, God does not teach Adam the animals' names; Adam "discovers" them himself. This proves important because for the Hebrew mind the naming of something was tantamount to perceiving its true nature. As Adam completes the task of naming, he realizes that while all the animals have mates, there is no animal in the creation that bears his nature and can serve as his mate. He experiences loneliness, and God steps in to create Eve as his equal partner. When Adam sees Eve, he exclaims with joy, "This *at last* is bone of my bone and flesh of my flesh" (Gen. 2:23, NRSV; italics added). In the Koranic account, however, the purpose of naming the animals is to shame the angels.

The Koran's account of the Fall morphs the serpent of Genesis 3 directly into Satan and fails to define the crucial nature of the forbidden tree. It also omits the process of the temptation of Eve and then Adam as well as the subsequent story of God's walking in the garden to find Adam, confronting them with their disobedience and then pronouncing judgment on the serpent, Eve, and Adam. Instead, we are given a brief synopsis of this whole account, which remains vague and unsatisfying without the biblical details.

Cain and Abel

Cain and Abel (Qabil and Habil) are upheld in the Koran as the first sons of Adam and his wife. Sura 5:27–31 relates the story of their sacrificial offerings to God. When Cain's is rejected, he declares to his brother, "I will surely kill you." Abel replies, "Truly, Allah accepts only from those who are among the pious," and he assures Cain that even if Cain seeks to kill him, he would never try to kill Cain, for he fears God. In fact, Abel becomes almost a willing partner to his own murder in order that Cain's fate in hell might be sealed! Cain carries through on his murderous threat and thereby stands with the number of the condemned.

While Abel's body is lying around in plain view, Allah amazingly shows Cain how to hide the body by sending before him a raven who has just lost its mate and scratches a hole in the ground to bury its dead partner. Cain experiences regret over the fact that he is not as smart even as this raven in discerning how to hide his brother's lifeless body. This account concludes with a moral that seems to bear a tenuous connection at best with what has preceded it: "Because of that, We ordained for the children of Israel that if anyone killed a person not in retaliation of murder, or to spread mischief in the land, it would be as if he killed all mankind. And if anyone saved a life, it would be as if he saved the life of all mankind" (5:32).

How are we to understand the connection between this moral and the story of Abel's murder? Interestingly, a similar story to the one told in 2:27–31 is found in Jewish Midrash predating Muhammad by hundreds of years. In the Jewish story, however, the main character is Adam, not Cain. We read in *Pirqe Rabbi Eliezer*:

> Adam and his companion [Eve] sat weeping and mourning for him [Abel] and did not know what to do with him as burial was unknown to them. Then came a raven, whose companion was dead, took its body, scratched in the earth, and hid it before their eyes; then said Adam, "I shall do as this raven has done," and at once he took Abel's corpse, dug in the earth, and hid it.

As to the cryptic moral in the Koranic account, another passage from Jewish literature clarifies its connection with the murder of Abel. Mishnah Sanhedrin 4:5 declares:

> For so we have found it with Cain that slew his brother, for it is written, "The bloods of your brother cry." It says not, "The blood of your brother," but "The *bloods* of your brother"—his blood and the blood of his posterity. . . . Therefore but a single man was created in the world, to teach that if any man has caused a single soul to perish, Scripture imputes it to him as if he had caused a whole world to perish; and if any man saves alive a single soul, Scripture imputes it to him as though he had saved alive a whole world.

In other words, the concluding moral found in the Koranic story of Abel's murder ultimately derives from a clever rabbinic interpretation of the parallel biblical text in Genesis 4:10, where the Hebrew word for blood is written in the plural. The Koran apparently conflates the biblical story of Cain and Abel with Jewish mythology and rabbinic teaching so as to produce, as from the mouth of Allah, the Islamic account of Qabil and Habil.

Noah and the Flood

Stories concerning the prophet Noah (Nuh) appear in numerous suras (7:59–64; 10:71–73; 11:25–48; 23:23–29; 26:105–20; 29:14–15; 71:21–28). According to 29:14–15 Noah lived among his people for 950 years as a prophet. Sura 71 presents a complaint from Noah to Allah about all the unbelievers who have scorned his message, followed by a plea that God might destroy them all to prevent them from leading astray the righteous in the future. Sura 11 contains a more detailed account of Noah's ministry, which is supplemented by brief, repetitious passages in other suras (7, 10, 23, 26, 29).

Noah has been sent from Allah, saying (in exactly the same phrasing as Muhammad uses among his own people), "I have come to you as a plain warner." His message to the people is that they should worship none but Allah. But the vast majority spurn Noah and mock his warnings. Allah comforts Noah and commands him to build the ark, confirming that Noah's enemies will remain in unbelief and suffer drowning as punishment. When the flood comes, Noah gathers two of every species, male and female, according to Allah's command. He also shepherds his family and the few other believers who have gathered around his message.

But one of Noah's sons refuses to believe and board the ark, determining instead to seek refuge on a mountain. As the mounting waves rise between Noah and his son, the son is drowned because of his unbelief. After an indeterminate time, the waters recede at the decree of Allah, and the ark comes to rest on a mountain called Judi. Noah then pleads with Allah for mercy on his dead son, saying he "is of my family." But Allah replies, "He is not of your family, for his conduct is unrighteous. So do not ask Me about that of which you have no knowledge" (11:46).

We see many parallels between the Koran's account of Noah and that of the Old Testament. Again, however, the Koranic version is often vague on details. Moreover, there are significant differences. Whereas the Koran reports word for word the mocking conversations between Noah and his opponents, Genesis is silent concerning *any* interactions between Noah and his contemporaries.[1] Likewise, Noah's cursing of the unbelievers before Allah in the Koran is absent in Genesis; Muhammad claims that Noah's wife (!) as well as one of his sons drowns because of unbelief, and that an unnamed, unnumbered group of believers were among those saved in the ark.

The Old Testament, however, asserts that all Noah's sons, his wife, and their wives alone were saved in the ark with Noah, with the rest of humanity destroyed. Interestingly, according to Muslim tradition Noah's unbelieving son is identified as Canaan, though the Bible identifies Canaan as the son of Ham and thus the grandson of Noah.

More important than these discrepancies, however, is the overarching theological intent present in the biblical account that drops out of the Koran. Muhammad tells the story to show how God sent Noah as a warner to his people. When they refused to embrace his message, God created a flood to destroy them. This implies that one may expect a similar judgment from Allah whenever his prophets are rejected by their people. But in the biblical account, the wickedness of the human race is already fully apparent to God before Noah's commission. Noah is not primarily a prophetic figure but a type of the Savior or Messiah, sent to save a remnant of humanity as the promise of a blessed future. The flood story ends not with a warning to present-day listeners of impending judgment for refusal to heed God's prophets, but rather with a gracious promise from God that he will never again destroy the earth by flood, a promise sealed in a covenant with creation, utilizing the sign of the rainbow. Mercy, not judgment, has the final word.

Lot and the Old Woman

The Koran's treatment of Lot demonstrates Muhammad's growing biblical accuracy over time as he apparently learns more of the biblical record from his Jewish and Christian contemporaries. As told by

Muhammad, Lot's rescue from Sodom parallels that of Genesis in most respects. The differences are notable at first, but the more the story is retold, the closer the accounts become. For instance, in the early renderings (Suras 26:160–75; 37:133–36), Lot warns the men of Sodom over God's impending wrath for their homosexual activity and prays that God will save him and his family from this judgment. Sura 26:170–71 reads, "So We saved him and his family all, except an old woman among those who remained behind" (see also 37:134–35, which repeats the same words). But in Sura 27:54–58, where a condensed version of the same story is given, the "old woman" is now clearly defined as Lot's wife (27:57).

In Sura 15:51–77, a still more detailed account of the destruction of Sodom appears—from the arrival of angelic visitors to Abraham announcing first the promise of a son being born miraculously to him and his barren wife, to the revelation of God's intention to destroy the valley of Sodom but save Lot and his family (minus his wife), to the actual visit of these guests in Lot's home and the attempted assault on them by Sodom's inhabitants, to the blindness of this mob and their ultimate destruction. In contrast to the biblical witness of Genesis 18:16–29, the angelic messengers announce to Abraham immediately their mission to rescue Lot from destruction. Upon their arrival in Sodom, they share privately with Lot this same mission, thereby revealing their true identity as angels.

This creates a curious plot twist when the mob shows up to demand the visiting "men" for their sexual pleasure. Angels can presumably take care of themselves, but Lot seeks to intervene on their behalf and protect his guests by offering his daughters to assuage the lusts of the crazed mob. We are not told in Sura 15 what happens after this offer, except that the crowd "in their wild intoxication were wandering blindly" until morning, when destruction overtook them.

This account is told once more in Sura 11:74–85, where the sequence of events is corrected: The visitors come, but they do not yet reveal to Lot their true nature or purpose. The crowd comes seeking to rape them, but Lot tries to prevent this abomination. The angels reveal their true nature and command Lot to flee with his family. Sodom is destroyed at daybreak. Strangely, no mention of blindness among the people is mentioned here, much less the biblical report that the blindness was the work of the angels so as to prevent the mob from acting on its lusts. Nonetheless, the account of Sura 11 preserves the integrity of the biblical (and logical) sequence, at the cost of undercutting the account in Sura 15.

Abraham

Mention of Abraham occurs more frequently in the Koran than that of any other prophet except Moses. After all, Muhammad identifies the message of Islam with the "religion of Abraham" (e.g., 2:130; 4:125; 16:122) and claims that Allah commanded the patriarch together with his son Ishmael to construct the sacred sanctuary in Mecca known now as the Ka'aba, considered Islam's holiest site (see 2:127; 3:95–97; 22:26). Abraham's prophetic message, according to Muhammad, was: "Worship Allah only, and fear Him" (29:16); shun all idols and submit to your only Helper. Muhammad holds Abraham up before his listeners as a model to emulate, one who worshiped Allah only, rejected idolaters in hatred (except his father, for whom he asked divine forgiveness[2]) until they should repent (60:4). As a reward for such obedience, Allah makes Abraham his friend (4:125) and a spiritual leader for the human race (2:124–25). Muhammad himself is commanded to follow in the footsteps of Abraham's monotheism.

Indeed, according to the Koran, when Abraham was engaged in building the Ka'aba and learning through revelation what were to be the properly ordained rituals for all pilgrims to Mecca, he prayed for the city that Allah would make it a place of peace and serenity, free from idol worship, and that someday in the future he would send a prophet to the people who would "recite the verses" and instruct the Meccans in the Book (i.e., the Koran) and in wisdom, thus leading them to purity. This prophetic prayer of Abraham was made known to the Meccans of Muhammad's day by Muhammad's own "revelations," and not surprisingly Muhammad claimed to be the fulfillment of the self-serving prophecy he attributed to Abraham.

The Koran relates four stories of Abraham's life, two of which are repeated numerous times in separate suras. The most prominent tale features a confrontation between Abraham and his father and countrymen. Versions of this story, which has no biblical parallel,[3] appear six times in the Koran (6:74–84; 19:41–49; 21:51–72; 26:69–89; 37:83–98; 43:26–27). The general plot involves Abraham disputing with these unbelievers over the futility of their idols, condemning their polytheism and extolling the virtues of Allah. His father and countrymen finally decide to get rid of Abraham by throwing him into a blazing fire, but Allah causes the fire to become cool and safe for Abraham and rewards him with the promise of faithful children, Isaac and Jacob.

In these six accounts we find varying details and emphases. For example, in 6:74–84, Abraham tries to convert his father (given the name Azar in this text[4]). In the context of this account, Abraham's own journey to monotheistic faith is recounted. Looking up into the sky, he places his faith consecutively in a bright star, the moon, and then the sun, only to watch each set in its turn and so prove itself unworthy of his worship. Only he who created these great lights can be unchanging and uncreated and thus worthy of human submission.

In 21:51–72, Abraham declares that when the unbelievers leave their temple of idols, he will plot to destroy the false gods. They leave, and he proceeds to smash all but the largest idol. When the unbelievers discover what has happened, Abraham naturally surfaces as the likely culprit. When interrogated, however, he denies his involvement and claims that the largest idol must be the guilty party. "Ask him," Abraham challenges them. After huddling to discuss their strategy, the idolaters respond to Abraham, "You know that our idols can't talk!" "Why then do you worship such useless things as gods?" Abraham retorts. At this affront, the unbelievers (including his father) seize him amidst cries from the crowd, "Burn him!" They build a red-hot fire and throw him in, but God miraculously protects his prophet by making the fire cool and peaceful for Abraham, who later walks forth unscathed.

The second major Koranic story involving Abraham relates his encounter with God's messengers on their way to destroy Sodom and Gomorrah (though these towns are never mentioned by name). Recounted in four locations (11:69–76; 15:51–60; 29:31–32; 51:24–34), this tale follows the biblical account in basic outline. Messengers of Allah on a journey arrive at Abraham's tent. He welcomes them and sets a meal of roasted calf before them. When they do not eat, however, he becomes alarmed with mistrust (11:70). The messengers reassure him of their benign intentions toward him. In Sura 51 they say, "Fear not, we bring you tidings of a wise son" (see also 15:51ff.). Sarah overhears this proclamation and responds in this account not with laughter but by crying out and striking her face while exclaiming, "A barren, old woman?!"

After this, Abraham presses the messengers as to the purpose of their journey (51:31; cf. 15:57). They unveil their intentions (and their identity as angels): "We have been sent to the guilty folk, to destroy by a hail of clay stones all those marked by the Lord for destruction, all except Lot and his family" (minus Lot's wife, who is of "those who stay behind" [15:60]). According to Sura 11, Abraham pleads for the "folk of Lot" (i.e., the inhabitants of Sodom and Gomorrah), but the angels say, "It is a matter already decided," and the debate ends there.

The order of the above events as found in Sura 11 differs markedly from that of Sura 51 at one significant point. In Sura 51 the angels reveal first God's promise of a son and then their purpose in coming to destroy Sodom and Gomorrah, but in Sura 11 the order is reversed. In both cases, Sarah's response to their words is recorded as happening between these two revelations. While in Sura 51 Sarah cries out understandably at the news of her upcoming pregnancy (though this falls short of the biblical response that clearly has her laughing incredulously at the news), in Sura 11 Sarah's laughter is linked not to the declaration of a promised son but to that of the destruction of the cities in the plain together with all their inhabitants.

Some Islamic commentators, troubled by this connection, argue that Sarah's laughter is a reaction of relief at the discovery that these messengers are indeed beneficent and thus not a threat to Abraham and her. Others seek to tie her laughter to the following revelation of her miraculous conception. But the Arabic grammar of this passage as well as the internal logic of the flow of the story do not lend themselves easily to such a rearrangement of order. What we are left with is an odd, if not macabre, instance of laughter with no connection to the original reason in the Bible for the recording of Sarah's laughter, which serves as the source and rationale for Isaac's name.[5] Additionally, we are faced with a troubling disparity in the divergent ways this story is told in the Koran, a book claimed by its adherents to be without error of any sort.

The third major story concerning Abraham is found only in Sura 37:100–107. Well-known in Jewish, Christian, and Muslim circles, this text tells in shorthand what is expressed in much greater detail in Genesis 22:1–19, namely, Abraham's willingness to sacrifice his son at God's command. There are interesting differences between the Koranic and biblical accounts. As told by Muhammad, this event takes place when Abraham's son (unnamed in Sura 37)[6] is old enough to accompany his father on a trip. Abraham reveals to his son a dream in which the patriarch slaughters his boy as an offering to Allah. He asks his son for his opinion concerning this dream, to which the lad replies, "Father, do what you are commanded; if Allah wills, I shall be obedient." Both of them submit themselves to Allah's will and so prepare for the sacrifice. Before they can carry out the act, however, Allah calls out to Abraham and says, "You have fulfilled the dream." Verse 107 then declares, "And We [Allah] ransomed him with a great sacrifice," paralleling the Genesis account of God's provision of a ram (caught by its horns in a nearby thicket) to serve as a ransom in place of Isaac.

For Christians, of course, this ransom bears tremendous typological significance, pointing forward to the matchless sacrifice of God in Christ as the ransom price paid to free us from the penalty of our sins. In Islam, the idea of ransom/sacrifice plays almost no role, except that the event of 37:100ff. is recalled every year in the slaying of an animal on the holy day of *Eid al-Adha* (lit., "the feast of sacrifice").

The final story in the Koran concerning Abraham finds no biblical counterpart and indeed seems rather anachronistic, even filled with fancy. In an age when the notion of life after death was murky at best, Abraham is said to cry out to God, "My Lord! Show me how you give life to the dead." Allah replies, "Do you not believe?" to which the patriarch quickly answers, " Yes, I believe, [but I ask in order] to satisfy my heart." Allah then commands Abraham, "Take four birds, then cause them to incline towards you (i.e., slay them and cut them into pieces), and then put a portion of them on every hill, and call them; they will come to you in haste. And know that Allah is almighty, all-wise" (2:260).

The principal sons of Abraham are mentioned in the Koran only in passing, often in lists with other prophets. Ishmael finds special mention as assisting Abraham in the construction of the Kaʾaba. Isaac's name occurs typically in conjunction with that of Jacob, implying that both are the offspring of Abraham. Presumably, Muhammad had often heard the triumvirate of patriarchal names (Abraham, Isaac, and Jacob) and, knowing Isaac to be Abraham's son, perhaps assumed that Jacob fell into the same category. This is only speculation, but it would make sense of passages in the Koran that are otherwise problematic.

The fact of Abraham's important role in the Koran and in Islamic tradition can provide a wonderful bridge for conversation between Christians and Muslims. I have engaged in many fruitful conversations with Muslim friends and acquaintances by investigating their understanding of the Koran's description of Abraham as the "friend of God" and relating to them that the Bible also refers to the patriarch in this way (2 Chron. 20:7; Isa. 41:8; James 2:23). While the Koran declares that this friendship is due to (and dependent on) Abraham's submissive obedience to the commands of Allah, the Bible instead emphasizes Abraham's trust in God's gracious promises.

Particularly in Romans 4, the apostle Paul makes clear that Abraham's justification as one righteous before God is a result not to his own efforts to earn God's favor but to God's pleasure over Abraham's trust in the many divine promises made to him. From this truth it is a small step to the realization that if Jesus Christ is the One in whom all the promises of God find their "Yes" and "Amen" (2 Cor. 1:20), then the way for human beings today to experience the justification of God and know his friendship is to put our full trust in Christ.

Knowing what the Koran has to say about biblical prophets both in terms of similarities and differences can become an effective bridge for opening conversations and friendships with Muslims. In the process, we will learn more deeply what moves the hearts and actions of our Muslim neighbors and develop natural entry points for sharing with them the good news of the gospel of Jesus Christ.

The streams of Judeo-Christian material flowing into the Koran do not end with Abraham and his sons. Indeed, some of Muhammad's most detailed accounts of biblical prophets are found in the lives of those who followed after Abraham. To these we will turn in the coming chapter.

CHAPTER

8

More Streams in the Desert:
Biblical Persons in the Koran

Around the kitchen table last month I had a lively discussion with two Muslim relatives about various religious figures. One of them was Jesus, whom they of course insisted was only a prophet. When I quoted them the words of Jesus as recorded in John 14:6 ("I am the way and the truth and the life; no one comes to the Father except through me"), one of them was horrified and adamantly claimed that the prophet Jesus would never say anything so blasphemous. While we did not come to a significant meeting of the minds in that conversation about Jesus (for more about these matters, see chapter 4), we found much we could agree upon related to other biblical figures, especially Joseph.

Joseph

The story of Joseph (Yusuf) is perhaps the most detailed of any Koranic story bearing a biblical parallel. Found exclusively in Sura 12 (entitled "Yusuf"), this account condenses the events of Joseph's life (covering Gen. 37–50) into roughly one hundred verses (12:4–100). The general order of the events of Joseph's life follow the biblical account, beginning with his dream of supremacy over his brothers and ending with the reunion with his father and family in Egypt, where Joseph becomes Pharaoh's right-hand man.

The discrepancies between this and the biblical report, however, prove interesting. When Joseph's brothers tell their father Jacob their concocted story of Joseph's death, Jacob does not believe them. Joseph is not sold to a passing caravan by the brothers, but he is thrown into a well and left for dead. A slave from a passing caravan, stopping to draw water, discovers him in the well, after which Joseph is taken down to Egypt and sold to an Egyptian slave master (Potiphar in the Bible but unnamed in the Koran). When the slave master's wife attempts to seduce Joseph and he flees from her advances, she grabs his shirt and tears it from behind. She then complains to her husband that Joseph assaulted her, but when he sees the evidence of Joseph's torn shirt (obviously grabbed from behind), the slave master believes Joseph rather than his wife!

The neighborhood women begin gossiping about the low morals of this wife, whereupon she invites them to a meal and parades Joseph before them. They are stunned by his handsome features and presumably now understand why the wife acted as she did. She in turn openly confesses to them her attempt at seduction and further declares, "Now if he refuses to obey my order (to sleep with her), he shall certainly be cast into prison" (12:32). Joseph, however, refuses again and so ends up in prison—for refusing to commit adultery!

The remainder of the story—Joseph's rise to power and his reunion with his brothers and father—parallels the biblical account except for one major difference: In the Koran, this is merely one more story of God's special favor bestowed on one of his prophets, whereas in the Bible, it occupies an important place in the flow of salvation history—that God sovereignly predestines the events of Joseph's life so as to put him in the powerful position of being able to save the lives of many, including his father and brothers (Gen. 50:20), and to move the descendants of the patriarchs to Egypt. This sets the stage for God's spectacular, redemptive work through Moses.

Moses

Of all the biblical prophets, Moses is the ultimate paragon for Muhammad. His name appears in the Koran far more often than that of any other prophet, and he seems to be the one after whom Muhammad styled his own ministry. For example, Muhammad speaks in summary fashion of Moses and Aaron as obedient slaves of Allah (37:114–22), mirroring his own passion. Furthermore, he likens the resistance and faithless questioning of his own people toward his mission to that of the unbelieving Jews toward Moses in Old Testament days (2:108).

The story of Moses' life is told and retold in numerous recitations. Again, the main story line follows that of Exodus and Numbers, in a highly condensed version and with some curious differences. The Koran adds two mysterious extrabiblical tales about Moses that lack any connection to the rest of Moses' life.

Sura 28:3–43 records how Moses' mother is inspired by Allah to put her infant son into the Nile and how Moses is rescued, taken to Pharaoh's court, and adopted—not by Pharaoh's daughter (as in the Bible) but by his wife. Moses grows up amid Egyptian royalty, but after killing a native citizen he flees to Midian. There he helps two sisters water their flock in the face of intimidation by certain male shepherds, and as a reward the girls' father offers one of them to Moses in marriage, provided Moses will commit to eight years in his service.

After those eight years, as Moses is traveling with his family, he espies a suspicious fire in the distance and goes off to investigate it. Here Allah reveals himself to Moses, not as "I am who I am" but simply as "I am Allah, the Lord of all." The fledgling prophet is told to throw down his stick, which becomes a snake, and then to place his hand in his bosom, which turns white (26:10ff; see also 22:7–14). After these signs, Allah commands Moses to go to Pharaoh to demand the release of the Jews. Moses complains that since he has killed an Egyptian, he is a marked man back in Egypt. Further, he suggests, Aaron is more eloquent.[1] Nonetheless, with Aaron as helper, Moses is sent to Pharaoh.

The confrontation with the king of Egypt is recounted often in the Koran (7:103ff.; 10:75–93; 17:101–4; 20:49ff.; 23:45–49; 26:16ff.; 43:46–55; 79:15–25) with slight variations. In front of the sorcerers of Egypt, who have been summoned by Pharaoh to contest Moses, the staff-turned-snake of the prophet swallows up the lesser snakes conjured up by Egyptian magic. As a result, the sorcerers repent of their unbelief and confess faith in Allah, to the great anger of Pharaoh, who threatens to cut off their opposing hands and feet and then crucify them.[2] Even this cannot dissuade them from their newfound faith.

In an intriguing side story, Pharaoh commands one of his advisors, named Haman,[3] to build a tower of clay-fired bricks that will scale to the heavens so that Pharaoh in his arrogance might ascend there to confirm that there is no God such as Moses claims (28:38–39; 40:36–38). Pharaoh and Haman are linked two other times (29:39; 40:23–24) with a third arrogant evildoer named Korah (Qarun). In Sura 40 we read, "Indeed we sent Moses with our signs and a manifest authority to Pharaoh, Haman and Korah, but they cried out, 'A sorcerer, a liar!'" Here it appears that Korah forms a part of the Egyptian court. Yet in a third passage mentioning Korah, we are told that he was a member of the people of Israel and was harshly judged by God for opposing Moses in the wilderness. The Bible also mentions Korah, but it limits his role to the leading of a rebellion among the Jews after their Exodus from Egypt (Num. 16).

In 40:23ff., Pharaoh declares his intention to personally kill Moses. But a member of Pharaoh's family, who is secretly a true believer, counsels Pharaoh in Gamaliel-like fashion to leave Moses alone, for if Moses' God is the real one, then Pharaoh will find himself facing fiery judgment. The king, however, refuses to listen, and through his power and position leads the people astray, in spite of the signs Moses performs (nine in all, according to the Koran). As a result, the Egyptians pursue the Jews to the edge of the sea, but Moses strikes the sea with his staff (26:63), it parts, and the people of God escape through the parted waters. When the Egyptians attempt to follow, God causes the waters to collapse on them, and Pharaoh and his army are drowned.

After the Exodus, the Jews are commanded by God to venture to the Holy Land, which he has assigned to them (5:21). Along the way, God calls Moses up to a mountain for forty nights (2:21f.; or "thirty nights plus ten added" [7:142]). Moses appoints Aaron to watch over the people, but in the prophet's absence they turn, under the influence of as-Samiri,[4] to the worship of an idol in the form of a calf, which appears to low. Meanwhile, on the mountaintop Moses asks to see God. Allah replies, "You cannot see me, but look instead at this mountain nearby as I show Myself to it." The mountain is pulverized to dust and Moses knocked unconscious. When he comes to, he repents of his audacity (7:143ff.).

Moses then returns to the valley and witnesses the idolatry of the Jews. Incensed, he calls Aaron to account. But God has already identified as-Samiri as the culprit. The people seek to excuse themselves, pretending that according to as-Samiri's instructions they simply threw their gold jewelry into a blazing fire and out came a golden calf. Moses demands their repentance, instructing the truly innocent to slay the guilty. Allah accepts this form of repentance, after which Moses ends the incident by banishing as-Samiri from the people.

Later, some of the people demand to see Allah as a condition for believing. In response, Allah kills them with a lightning bolt, but then immediately restores them to life that they might show him appropriate gratitude (2:55–56)! Some among the Jews continue to show their unbelief by transgressing the Sabbath. Because of this, Allah punishes them by transforming them into apes, as a lesson to coming generations (2:65–66).

As the people experience thirst in the wilderness, God commands Moses to strike a rock with his staff. This results in twelve springs gushing forth from the rock, one for each of the tribes of Israel (2:60; see also 7:160).

Finally, Moses and the Israelites reach the banks of the Jordan, poised to enter the land God has commanded them to possess. However, the people balk because of rumors that there are "people of great strength in the land." Two unnamed men (Joshua and Caleb in the Bible) urge the people to trust in Allah and go to battle, but the people tell Moses there is no way they will cross the Jordan until the fearsome inhabitants have been removed. They urge Moses to venture over with God and fight while they watch in safety. For this cowardice, Allah judges the people with forty years of wandering before granting Israel access to the Promised Land (5:20–26).

The Koran tells two last stories about Moses that have no biblical parallel and seem devoid of any historical basis or connection with his prophetic ministry. In Sura 2:67–71, Moses tells the people that God is commanding them to slaughter a cow. The people ask God to be clearer regarding the kind of cow to be sacrificed. Moses answers, "It must not be too old or too young." The people press further. "What color?" The prophet tells them it must be bright yellow. Not yet satisfied, the people probe further. Moses finally declares, "It must be healthy, only yellow, not trained to till the soil or water the fields." "Ah," the people say (translated into our vernacular), "now you're talking." And they slaughter the appropriate cow.

In the second story, Sura 18:60–82 records a perplexing story, one difficult to interpret meaningfully. Moses and a young servant are traveling until they reach the junction of two seas (apparently a long journey). When they arrive and sit down to rest, a live fish they have been carrying for food apparently escapes unnoticed into the sea and disappears. After a brief rest, the men continue their long journey before setting up camp. Moses commands the young servant to prepare the fish they have brought for their breakfast. When the servant discovers there is no fish, he confesses to Moses that he forgot the fish back at the junction. Indeed, the servant says, "Satan made me forget."

So Moses and the servant retrace their steps, and by Allah's providence encounter one of Allah's servants (unnamed in the Koran, but known as Khidr in Islamic tradition). Moses recognizes his wisdom and pleads to become his disciple. Khidr replies that Moses doesn't have enough patience to remain with him for long. But Moses responds, "If

Allah wills, I will not disobey you in anything." Khidr relents on one condition, that Moses not question him about anything until Khidr himself brings up the subject. Moses agrees to this stipulation.

As they begin their journey together, they come to a sailing ship and board it. But Khidr immediately damages the ship so severely as to scuttle it. Moses accuses him of evil: "Are you not trying to drown these people? Surely that is evil!" Khidr replies, "Did I not tell you that you would have no patience?" Moses then apologizes for forgetting his pledge. Continuing their journey, they soon meet a boy. Khidr kills him, with no explanation. Moses again erupts, questioning Khidr's goodness. Again Khidr reminds Moses of his lack of patience and the breaking of his vow, and Moses repents a second time.

Finally, they come to a village and request food from the inhabitants but are refused. While still in the town, Khidr discovers a stone wall about to collapse and repairs it free of charge. Moses complains, noting that surely such work is worthy of payment (at least in exchange for some food). Khidr has had enough of Moses' impatience and determines that they must part ways. But first he explains his mysterious behaviors to Moses. The ship, we are told, was owned by a collective of poor people and was about to be seized as booty by a powerful king. In scuttling it, Khidr foiled the king's plans and yet made it possible for the people to repair it at relatively little expense. The boy he killed was rebellious and disbelieving toward his parents and so was a great hardship on them. Allah will grant these parents another son, who will be more righteous. The wall in the village was part of some property owned by two orphans whose father had been a God-fearing man. Under the area sheltered by the wall was a great treasure that Allah wanted the boys to have as compensation for such a good father, but it never would have been discovered if the wall had collapsed.

The account ends with Khidr's observation that he did not do these things of his own accord but only as Allah directed. Moses' impatience kept him from discerning the deeper purposes of Allah in the seemingly meaningless or even evil events.

By and large, though the highlights of Moses' ministry are recounted in reports sprinkled throughout the Koran, little is recorded of the actual teachings that Moses brought the Israelites. The tablets of the law that God gives Moses for the people are mentioned, but nothing is revealed of their contents. Moses is said to have been given a book of revelation for Israel, but its details remain unspoken. Most likely this happens for two reasons: (1) Muhammad had no firsthand access to the Pentateuch in a language he could read; and (2) he assumed the revelation given to Moses would be essentially the same as what he proclaimed, so there was no need to explore the main prophetic work of Moses as lawgiver.

Other Biblical Characters

Elijah

The name of Elijah (Elias) occurs in a short list of prophets found in 6:85. Curiously, he is without explanation lumped together with the New Testament figures Zechariah and his son John (the Baptist), and Jesus, even though Elijah's ministry preceded the others by some eight hundred years.[5] The one substantive statement in the Koran concerning Elijah's ministry is found in 37:123–30, where as prophet he calls the people to account for worshiping the idol Baal instead of fearing Allah. Unfortunately, the people largely reject him, "except for the chosen slaves of Allah" (v. 128).

Elisha

Elijah's successor, Elisha, merits only two passing references (6:86; 38:48) in short lists of prophets who are described as among Allah's best servants.

Job

Muhammad apparently assumes significant knowledge of the story of Job on the part of his listeners, for Job himself receives only two short references, noting his patience (21:83–85) and Allah's mercy to him when he cried out for relief from his suffering (38:41–44). In the latter passage, Allah tells Job to "strike the ground" with his foot, as the result of which a spring of cool water wells up for him to wash and refresh himself.

Allah also restores to Job his family and fortune and issues to him an odd command: "Take in your hand a bundle of thin grass and strike therewith (your wife), and break not your oath" (38:44). This apparently links back to the story (unreported in the Koran) of Job's wife suggesting that he curse God and die. According to Islamic tradition, Job became angry at her advice and swore an oath to lash her one hundred times. God now is ordering Job to fulfill his oath, but in a merciful manner by using soft grass as the whip.

Jonah

In Sura 37:139–48 the story of Jonah (Yunus) is told in bare-bones fashion, and his name is mentioned elsewhere in two lists of prophets (4:163; 6:86). His flight from God is reported, the casting of lots to throw him overboard, his time in the belly of a great fish, and his regurgitation onto shore after repentance (see 21:87). Strangely, at this point Allah causes a gourd plant to grow over Jonah to shield him from the sun as he recuperates from illness caused by his sojourn in the fish. After this, Jonah is sent to "a hundred thousand people or even more" (37:147), an odd statement to come out of the mouth of an all-knowing God. Through Jonah's preaching, the people believe and are spared judgment for a time. The Koran never tells us who these people are to whom Jonah goes. From the biblical witness, we might assume Muhammad to mean the Ninevites, but Sura 10:98 simply refers to them as "the people of Jonah."

Saul

Israel's first king, Saul (Talut), is the focus of 2:246–49. The people of Israel ask an unnamed prophet (Samuel in the Bible) to appoint for them a king, after which they will be willing to engage in *jihad* for Allah. However, when Saul is appointed, they balk, complaining that he is not rich enough or fit enough to be their king. The prophet responds that

Allah will show them a sign by bringing into their midst the ark of the covenant, carried by angels. The people then relent. Saul subsequently gathers his army and takes them to a river before battle. All those who drink *except* by raising water to their lips in the hollow of their hand are sent home (a conflation with the biblical account of Gideon, found in Judges 7:4–8?). The rest venture forth against the enemy, Goliath and his hosts.

David

David (Dawood), who occupies such a central role in Israel's history and hopes, finds mention at the end of this account as the one who kills Goliath and receives the kingdom after the death of Saul (see also 2:251). The Koran also identifies David as the prophet to whom Allah gave the book of Psalms (Zabur), the military leader to whom he gave the gift of making iron supple (so as to create coats of mail for his army [34:10–11]), and the sage to whom he gave the submission of all birds assembled in his service. Sura 5:78 speaks of David and Jesus as both cursing the Jews who strayed from the true path.

The longest Koranic story about David finds its source in the biblical account of the prophet Nathan's rebuke of David over his sin with Bathsheba (2 Sam. 12:1–15). In the Koran, however, Nathan is absent from the scene, and the parable he tells to trap David in his sin becomes an historical event (Sura 38:21–26). Two men with a complaint come to David seeking his wise judgment between them. The stronger, with ninety-nine sheep, has demanded of the weaker his lone ewe. Immediately David, without listening to the other side, takes up the cause of the weaker man and judges on his behalf. Somehow from this event, David discerns that God is convicting him of sin (though we are told nothing of his transgressions related to Bathsheba), and he prostrates himself in repentance.

Solomon

Solomon (Sulaiman) receives somewhat extended treatment in the Koran. He carries the wisdom of his father, David, and is blessed with even greater powers from Allah. He judges impeccably among the poor, learns also the art of working with metal for military purposes, is granted supernatural power over the winds to make them do his bidding (transporting him and his armies wherever he pleases), and has authority over demons (*jinn*) to use them as his servants (21:79–82; see also 34:12–13). According to 27:16, the language of birds was revealed to Solomon, and he commanded armies composed of men, *jinn*, and birds.

On one occasion, his armies are on the move across a valley. The Koran records the sharp warning of an ant to her fellow colony members on the valley floor as she espies the approaching columns: "O ants! Enter your dwellings, lest Solomon and his hosts should crush you, while they perceive not." Solomon overhears her speech and smiles in amusement (27:17–19).

Immediately following this account, Solomon inspects the gathered birds of his court and notices that one, the hoopoe, is missing. Upset, he resolves to punish the bird unless it has a compelling excuse for its absence. The bird appears and reveals to Solomon something he did not know. The hoopoe claims to have been to Sheba and discovered a race of wealthy people ruled by a queen with a great throne. Satan has barred them from knowledge of Allah and so they are sun worshipers.

Solomon determines to test the hoopoe's claims by commanding it to deliver a letter from him to the people of Sheba. When the queen reads the letter, which summons the people to appear before Solomon and submit to Allah, she asks her advisors for wisdom. Confident of their military strength, they cite the country's readiness to fight, but they leave the final decision in the queen's hands. With good discretion, the queen opts to send Solomon a gift to see how he responds, but Israel's king rejects the present, saying to the messengers, "Will you help me in wealth? What Allah has given me is better than what he has given you" (27:36). He orders them to return to Sheba, warning that he will come with his armies in due time to overpower them.

Then Solomon, anticipating the queen's surrender, turns to his chiefs and asks, "Who will bring me the queen's throne before they arrive?" An *efreet* (one of the leaders among the *jinn*) boasts that he can bring it to Solomon before the king dismisses his council. But apparently that is not soon enough for Solomon. Another ("with whom was knowledge of the Book") then declares, "I will bring it in the twinkling of an eye." So it is done. Solomon then orders the throne to be disguised so as to discover whether the queen will recognize it or not when she arrives. This apparently serves as a test to discern whether she is rightly guided by Allah or not. As the queen is ushered in, she is asked, "Is your throne like this?" To this she responds, "As if the very same."

Somehow Solomon concludes from this that she is not yet a Muslim. The queen is invited to enter his palace, which contains floors of clear glass. Having never seen anything like this before, the queen thinks instead that the floor is covered with water. So she lifts her robes and exposes her legs, preparing to wade across the room. Cryptically, when Solomon discloses to her that the floor is glass, she exclaims, "My Lord! Verily, I have wronged myself and I submit to Allah" (27:44; the entire account is found in 27:16–44).

The Koran records Solomon's great love for well-bred horses in 38:30–40. One day while inspecting some particularly stunning war steeds, he loses track of time until evening, neglecting his prayers. Allah apparently punishes Solomon by placing a look-alike demon on the king's throne in his stead, thereby supplanting him for a while. Solomon pleads for forgiveness, which Allah grants. Later, Allah also grants Solomon authority over the wind and the *jinn* to serve him, as a result of which (according to 34:12–13) he is able to travel two month's distance in a day on the wings of the wind and to create beautiful objects through the efforts of the enslaved *jinn*.

Muhammad's version of Solomon's death is recorded in 34:14. The king apparently dies while standing or leaning on his staff, but no one (including his family or courtiers) realizes this for quite some time (perhaps months or more), until a little worm has gnawed completely through his staff, causing it and him to collapse. The delayed discovery of Solomon's death is particularly galling to the *jinn*, who have continued slaving away in their servitude only because they assumed he was still alive!

John the Baptist

The vast majority of the biblical characters cited by Muhammad come from the Old Testament. Other than significant references to Mary and Jesus, the Koran is virtually silent on the people and events of the Gospels and early church. Only John the Baptist and his father Zechariah receive mention by name.

Sura 19:2–15 relates the story of Zechariah's secret prayer for a son despite his old age and his wife's barrenness. Allah announces to him the promise of a son to be called John (Yahya), but Zechariah wants a divine sign to confirm that this will indeed come to pass. Allah declares that for three days and nights (see also 3:38–41), the father-to-be will not be able to speak. After the birth, John grows up obedient and faithful to his parents and Allah, evidencing wisdom from his youth. Muslim tradition recognizes John the Baptist's role as a forerunner to Jesus, but the Koran itself gives only a veiled hint of this.[6]

Story of the Table

Two final stories in the Koran bear links to the age of the church (both New Testament and postapostolic), though they have no canonical roots. The first is found in 5:112–15, where the disciples of Jesus ask him whether Allah will send down a table from heaven spread with a feast for them. Jesus warns them not to presume, but they answer that such a miracle will strengthen their faith and confirm Jesus' claims as a prophet. So Jesus prays, and Allah grants his request, but with a severe warning to the disciples: "If any of you after that disbelieves, then I will punish him with a torment such as I have never before inflicted on anyone" (5:115).

There are no clear precursors for this story in any known literature, but it is entirely possible that Muhammad misunderstood the Christian phrase "the Lord's table" and perhaps conflated it with material from Psalm 78:19 or with the story of the feeding of the five thousand in the Gospels. The Arabic word used here for "table" (*ma'idah*) is found only here in the Koran and was originally derived from a similar Ethiopian word used by the native Abyssinian Christians as a technical term for the Lord's table (i.e., communion).

Story of the Young Men and a Dog in a Cave

Finally, we turn to a Koranic story with strong parallels in Christian apocryphal writings. Known colloquially as "The Companions of the Cave," this tale is recorded in 18:9–26. It concerns a group of young men and a dog who, fleeing from unbelievers, take refuge in a cave and pray for Allah's protection. Allah puts them into a deep sleep and awakens them three hundred (or three hundred and nine) years later. Interestingly, although Allah purports to narrate this story to Muhammad, there is uncertainty regarding the number of men he saved. Verse 22 declares that some say it was three, others five, some even seven. Either Allah is unsure himself (something impossible in Muslim thought), or for some unknown reason he refuses to clarify this minor detail.

A fascinating parallel to this account, written at least two hundred years before the beginning of Muhammad's revelations, is found in *Acta Sanctorum*, an apocryphal Christian work highlighting God's faithfulness to persecuted Christians. In this story, known informally as "The Seven Sleepers," Christians fleeing persecution during the reign of Decius (d. A.D. 251) huddle in a cave near Ephesus. The cave entrance is sealed for almost two hundred years, and the group falls into a deep sleep. When the cave is finally unsealed, the sleepers awake and one ventures forth into the nearby city. He is astonished to learn that in the intervening two centuries, the Roman empire has become largely Christianized, a far cry from the anti-Christian stance it had adopted prior to their period of hibernation. The emperor learns about them and comes to meet them at the cave. Joyfully, the men relate how God preserved them from martyrdom so as to serve as witnesses of his faithful protection. After glorifying God in this manner, they pass away.

Germ Seed

Though by no means an exhaustive treatment of all biblical characters and references in the Koran, these two chapters chronicle the biblical figures who find significant mention in the Koran, as well as events and circumstances that the Koran attaches to Jewish and Christian history apart from any mention in the Bible. As we have seen, most of the Koranic accounts dealing with the Bible contain at least the germ seed of the prior biblical material in their telling. However, we have also seen that many of the Koranic stories of biblical prophets lack strong historical anchors or logical sequence from story to story. The frequent lists of prophets often carry no discernible order, chronological or otherwise.

Apart from the laconic treatment of Jonah, the later Jewish prophets (from the eighth century B.C. onward) go unmentioned in the Koran. A number of stories found in Muhammad's revelations are traceable to earlier noncanonical accounts in the Jewish Talmud and Christian apocrypha. Names of some of the prophets, such as Jonah, Elijah, and Isaac, appear in the Arabic of the Koran as transliterations from their Greek forms (as would be expected if Muhammad received his information from Hellenized Jews and Christians) rather than being modeled on their original Semitic forms (as might be expected if these accounts were truly divinely revealed).

Soaked Up from Existing Muddy Streams

In the end, it seems fair to conclude that Muhammad, desiring to maintain conformity with what he believed was prior revelation from the true God, soaked up as much knowledge as he could from the streams of Jewish and Christian sources available to him in the western Arabian Peninsula. Unfortunately, these streams were often muddied themselves, as the native Jewish and Christian tribes were often uneducated and unschooled in their own holy texts. What Muhammad learns is often adulterated and riddled with gaps, and it was left up to him to piece things together with little or no prior understanding of the flow of biblical history.

In the midst of hearsay and secondary tributaries of material as well as in cultural surroundings used to the telling of fantastic tales, Muhammad rearranges much of what he had accumulated, sometimes conflating stories, sometimes mixing sources, all from the desire to undergird his claim to be a true prophet of God in line with the true prophets of old. Casting those former prophets in his image as harbingers of God's wrath against unbelief and polytheism, Muhammad sought to bolster the force of his own message and to compel listeners to a fateful decision: to side with Allah and his prophet, or to be against them.

Although Muhammad's goal to eradicate polytheism and immorality is laudable, a reasonable person looking at the Koran's use of biblical material would have to conclude that the Koran is a flawed document historically. As such, it cannot sustain the claim to be divinely inspired and without error. The streams in the desert from which Muhammad drank his theology and history were not pure enough to keep his message in line with that which God had revealed over the previous two thousand years to Israel and the church. One wonders whether, if Muhammad had been able to read Greek or Syriac or Latin and had had access to the Bible for himself, his message might have changed. Instead of becoming the founder of a new religion, he may have become an apostle of Christ to the Arabian Peninsula! This side of eternity we will never know, but one may always wonder.

The Agony and the Ecstasy: Hell and Heaven

On the theme of divine judgment, the Koran and the Bible share a similar, though not identical, outlook. According to both, the human race faces an intractable problem because God has established universal laws of moral right and wrong, which human beings without exception have transgressed. God is obligated by his sovereignty and justice to punish these transgressions, some at least of which are so serious as to merit an eternity of suffering in hell. Though God has a forbearing nature, delaying judgment out of mercy, one day he must call all human beings to account. That day, according to both the Bible and the Koran, will take place at the end of human history, when God brings this present creation to an end as he sits on the great throne of judgment and separates the righteous from the wicked—the blessed to dwell in everlasting glory in the new heavens and earth, the damned to exist in everlasting torment and desolation.

The Christian Solution to the Problem of the Human Race

The future of every mortal is in jeopardy because of the reality of sin—our disobedience toward or rebellion against God. According to the Bible this is an insurmountable problem for the human race because our battle is not just with acts of disobedience here and there for which we might seek to atone, but with an intransigent inner nature that remains corrupted and beyond our ability to cure. It is as if the steering system of our spirits is always out of alignment so that even though we think we may desire to seek after God, we always veer off the path, pursuing instead our own fallen desires or false gods.

For Christians, the situation is hopeless. We are not able to save ourselves, nor is there anything else in a fallen creation that can adequately come to our aid before a holy God. If we are to survive divine judgment, the solution will have to come from outside creation—indeed, from God himself. Thus, we are caught in a dilemma. The God of moral perfection we run from in fear, but that same God of love is our only hope of salvation. Fortunately, God has undone this dilemma for us by taking the initiative to intervene on our behalf as Savior.

The gospel of Jesus Christ is indeed "good news" because God the Son enters the turbulent line of human history to deal with sin and judgment by becoming one of us and by taking on his divine-human shoulders the weight of all sin through his sacrificial death at Calvary. He invites all sinners to exchange their sins for his righteousness at the cross and to experience the birth of a redeemed human nature through his resurrection life. In the gospel, the adamantine holiness of God is satisfied as his wrath is poured out justly on the sins borne by his Son, and the compassionate mercy of God the Father is displayed as he rescues those who have taken refuge under the atoning cross of his beloved Son. The God of justice before whom we once cowered in fear now beckons us to run into his outstretched arms of saving love.

The Muslim Solution of Repentance

For Islam, of course, the solution offered is different. Muslims reject the idea that human beings are radically alienated from God by a corrupt nature that cannot be overcome by our own efforts. Our natures are basically good, but they are weak. We easily fall into disobedience through forgetfulness of God's commands or the unwillingness to discipline our desires, but these problems can be corrected by the regimen revealed through the prophet Muhammad. The five daily prayers, the month of fasting, the regular giving of alms, the lifelong goal of a pilgrimage to Mecca with its plethora of somber rituals and requirements are all ways of training the mind and heart not to forget our duties to Allah.

Equally important, the fear of divine judgment consigning one to an eternity of despairing agony and the wish to be included instead among the righteous in a paradise of eternal sensual delights serve as powerful motivators to the prescribed behaviors of Islam. The theme of divine judgment finds a prominent place in the Koran (second only to the emphasis on the unique sovereignty of Allah), warning humanity to toe the line or face dire consequences. For Muslims, then, sin, though serious, is not an insurmountable problem, for it can be eradicated by repentance and hope in God's mercy for those who strive zealously to live in obedience to Allah. In this scenario, the holiness of God is subjugated to his mercy, as sins are not atoned for but rather swept under the rug of Allah's sovereign will for those whom he determines to forgive.

These teachings, unfortunately, leave Muslims with a deep uncertainty about their eternal destiny. While the Koran speaks often of Allah as the All-Forgiving, All-Compassionate One, no Muslim can be sure that such mercy will ultimately be directed toward him or her. Mercy itself is not part of God's nature but simply one of the ways he chooses in his freedom to act, just as wrath is another equally likely way he may freely choose to act. No one may presume that God will of necessity be kind to him or her. Even Muhammad voiced uncertainty over his own destiny as he recognized Allah's absolute freedom to act however he pleased.

The best Muslims can hope for is that by striving to live as obediently as possible (though in reality no one lives consistently to this degree), Allah may be moved to mercy by their relative merits when he weighs their lives in the divine balance. Were you to ask even the most devout Muslim whether he or she feels sure of reaching paradise upon death, the traditional response is *Inshallah!* ("If God is willing"). Perhaps Allah's forgiveness will tilt toward those characterized by Islamic piety in their hearts and submission to Allah in their deeds.

Islam's Day of Judgment

Muslims agree heartily with the sentiment of Hebrews 9:27: "Man is destined to die once, and after that to face judgment." Islam contains no hint of reincarnation or of a state of purgatory after death through which to purge one's earthly sins. Rather, the condition of one's soul at death (with all its recorded deeds, both good and evil) is that to which one must answer before the judgment seat of God. As to what happens between the time of one's death and the eschatological Day of Judgment, the Koran is largely silent, but most Islamic scholars hold that the soul continues in a state of sleep and experiences a mild foretaste of its ultimate destiny until finally reunited with the body in the general resurrection of all the dead,[1] immediately prior to the Great Judgment: "And the trumpet will be blown and behold from the graves they will come out quickly to their Lord. They will say: "Woe to us! Who has raised us from our place of sleep?" (Sura 36:51–52).

This Day of Judgment is never far from Muhammad's thoughts. It figures prominently in his warnings, and references to it, under various descriptive names, are sprinkled liberally through the Koran and Hadith traditions. It is:

- the Last Day
- the Day of Standing Up (i.e., the Resurrection)
- the Day of Separation (of the righteous from the wicked)
- the Day of Reckoning (of all accounts before Allah)
- the Day of Awakening (from sleep to the awareness of one's ultimate destiny)
- the Day of Encompassing (of all the deeds of all humankind in judgment).

Frequently, this eschatological event is called simply "the Hour" (6:31; 7:187; 15:85; 16:77; 22:1; 54:46), though the Koran envisions its actual length variously as one thousand years (32:5) or fifty thousand years (70:4). No one but Allah knows the time of its onset (according to one tradition, even Gabriel confesses ignorance when Muhammad presses him for more information). Nonetheless, Islamic tradition has developed a series of greater and lesser signs that must precede its arrival. The sudden and final sign will be the blast of a celestial trumpet, irresistibly summoning all creatures to the place of judgment—a location presumably situated on the newly recreated earth, though no human being knows where that will be (see 14:48).

The Koran clearly teaches that every person must stand alone in the tribunal before Allah. No one can serve as an intercessor or mediator for anyone else: "And fear the Day when one person shall not avail another, nor will intercession be accepted from him, nor will compensation be taken from him, nor will they be helped" (Sura 2:48).

Muhammad as a Savior Figure?

No doubt Muhammad knew of the Christian claims concerning the role of Jesus Christ as intercessor before God on behalf of those who placed their trust in his sacrifice. Therefore, he sought to dismiss this mediatorial work revealed in the Bible as well as any other savior figure to whom his listeners might appeal. In a fascinating contradiction to this clear teaching from the Koran, Islamic tradition has increasingly attempted to refashion Muhammad's own ministry from that of being simply a warner of impending judgment to that of a savior figure himself, recast along the lines of the church's claims for Jesus Christ.

One tradition reports that when Allah appears to judge the human race, Muhammad will step forward to assume the role of intercessor for all Muslims. This role will already have been declined by Adam, Noah, Abraham, Moses, and Jesus, all of whom (except Jesus, interestingly!) will cite particular sins they have committed that disqualify them from such a role. In popular Muslim tradition Muhammad is regarded as sinless, though the Koran clearly acknowledges his sins and calls him to repentance, like all other mortals.

Descriptions of the Day of Judgment are most lurid in the earlier suras of Muhammad's career, when he was most concerned to warn unbelievers of the danger of their condition apart from his unfolding message of Islam. Sura 75 (named "The Resurrection") warns those denying the resurrection that such denials will not prevent them from facing Allah's judgment after death. He will reconstitute them to face his wrath whether they choose to believe that or not. In that day, men will reel as the sun and moon are joined together (in eclipse) and light fails (75:7–9).

Suras 81–84 continue this apocalyptic imagery as on the Day of Resurrection the sun fails and the stars fall from the sky, the seas rage uncontrollably or blaze like fire, animals huddle together in terror, and the mountains are laid low. Muhammad adds a bit of indigenous Arab imagery to this description by declaring that on this day even pregnant she-camels (the most prized of possessions) will be neglected as their owners focus completely on self-survival. On this day, the books of deeds are laid open, hell is set ablaze, paradise is brought near, and everyone discovers his or her fate.

Unbelievers are reminded in Sura 82 that angels are busy recording each and every deed of every mortal, and on the Day of Recompense, when all graves are turned upside-down, none will be left in death but all will be raised to answer for their deeds before Allah alone.

Merchants who defraud customers with faulty scales and measures will not succeed in their subterfuge (Sura 83). Allah is not mocked, and these sins as recorded in detail by the angels will be fully punished. While unbelievers may now revel in their sins and belittle the faithful, the tables will be turned on the Last Day, when believers, seated on their high thrones, will look down on the faithless and laugh (83:34–35).

To all these images, Sura 84 adds that when the heavens are split asunder and the earth stretched forth, every human being will be handed the record of his or her life. Those receiving their book in their right hand will enjoy an easy reckoning and the reward of paradise. Those receiving their book behind their back (or in the left hand) will taste the burning fires of hell in lasting torment.

Among the later revelations, Sura 22:1–7 paints fresh scenes of terror. In panic, nursing mothers will forget their suckling babes, pregnant women will miscarry, and human beings in general will stagger as if in drunken stupor. False gods will be of no avail to polytheists, for these entities will themselves bear witness against their followers in submission to Allah. "Surely the hour is coming, there is no doubt about it," declares Muhammad (22:7). As God's judgment is rendered, creatures will be sent to one of two final destinations, hell or paradise. The Koran repeatedly describes both in vivid detail.

Descriptions of the Last Day and Hell

The overwhelmingly consistent image for hell in the Koran is fire. In fact, the word most often used to refer to hell is *an-Nar* ("the Fire"). According to tradition, the fires of hell burn seventy times hotter than earthly flames. It is the place of eternal torment. Known also as *Jahannum*,[2] it serves a purgatorial as well as a judicial role. Islam teaches that all human beings must at least pass through if not remain in hell (19:71). The pious Muslims will be rescued from it and established in paradise, while the rest will continue in its perpetual flames.

According to 15:44, hell has seven gates or levels, one for each class of sinners. Muslim teachers traditionally draw the name of each level from the various titles for hell found in the Koran, though there is no warrant for this from the texts themselves. On this model, *Jahannum* is the first and "mildest" level, the site where all Muslims sojourn for a time before being gathered to paradise, should they be so fortunate. The second level, known as *Latha*, is reserved for Christians[3] (70:15–18). Through the third gate pass the Jews into *al-Hutamah*, with its "crushing fire" (104:4–7). *Sa'ir*, the fourth level, is reserved for the Sabeans (or Zoroastrians; see 4:10, one of twelve occurrences of the term). The fifth hell, known as *Saqar*, will be set apart for the Magi and all polytheists: "That day they will be dragged on their faces into the Fire: 'Taste you the touch of *Saqar!*'" (54:48; see also 74:42). Idolaters will be gathered into the next to lowest spot, *al-Jahim*, while the most terrible of all torments, *Hawiyah* ("the Pit") will be the living nightmare of all "hypocrites," that is, those who once embraced Islam and then turned away in apostasy.

In Muhammad's early suras, hell serves primarily as the penalty for those who reject the prophet's mission. Unbelievers, without regard to their moral stature, are warned of the fate reserved for all who scorn God's apostle. In Sura 74:11–26, for instance (the second revelation given by Muhammad), Allah singles out one Meccan unbeliever (al-Walid ibn al-Mughirah al-Makhzumi) who was leading early opposition to Muhammad and sealed his fate in hell for this.

The Vulnerability of Women

In later suras, the justification for the penalties of hell widens beyond opposition of the prophet to include a broad list of sins such that no human being is beyond the reach of divine judgment. Women seem especially vulnerable. Though not often mentioned directly in the Koran's teachings on hell, in popular Islamic tradition women are in greater spiritual peril than men. Although Sura 4:1 offers the hope of paradise to anyone male or female who "does righteous good deeds and is a true believer," the Hadith traditions paint a different and grimmer picture for the female gender. Muhammad relates that one woman who had kept a cat locked up till it died of hunger was doomed to the tortures of hell because of this transgression (al-Bukhari 3:323). Even more disheartening, though, is the following often-repeated tradition:

> Once Allah's Apostle went out to the Musalla [to offer the prayer] of Eid al-Adha or al-Fitr prayer. Then he passed by the women and said, "O women! Give alms, as I have seen that the majority of the dwellers of hell-fire were you." They asked, "Why is it so, O Allah's Apostle?" He replied, "You curse frequently and are ungrateful to your husbands. I have not seen anyone more deficient in intelligence and religion than you." The women asked, "O Allah's Apostle! What is deficient in our intelligence and religion?" He said, "Is not the evidence of two women equal to the witness of one man?" They replied in the affirmative. He said, "This is the deficiency in your intelligence. Isn't it true that

a woman can neither pray nor fast during her menses?" The women replied in the affirmative. He said, "This is the deficiency in your religion." (al-Bukhari, 1:181–82)

Descriptions of Hell

Lurid descriptions of hell regularly color the pages of the Koran. It blazes with insatiable flames that crackle and roar (25:14). Dense, black smoke roils and scorching winds buffet the wicked (56:42–44). Scalding waters boil uncontrollably (55:44) as hell bursts with fury (67:7–8). Its hunger for more inhabitants is voracious; in 50:30 we are told that one day Allah will say to hell, "Are you filled yet?" and hell will respond, "Are there yet more to come?" The damned will suffer endlessly the agonies of burning flesh and scalded throats. They will be forced to wear garments of fire or pitch (14:50) and to endure so many boiling fluids poured down over their heads that their skins as well as the contents of their bellies will melt (22:19–20).

In order that their agonies may always be fresh, "as often as their skins are roasted through, We [Allah] shall change them for other skins that they may taste the punishment" (4:56). Though they will plead for extinction, they will not be permitted to die a second death so as to escape this eternal misery (14:17). Their only libations will be foul, boiling water followed by icy draughts of a dark, murky liquid. For food they will be fed the pus of festering wounds (69:36; 78:25) or the demonic fruit of the bitter Zaqqum tree, whose roots feed off the deepest fires of hell (37:62–67). Bound by chains seventy cubits in length, they will endure the weight of eternal shackles (69:30–32). Pleas to the angelic sentinels for mercy will fall on deaf ears; all that awaits their future is ever-increasing torment (78:30).

As if these Koranic images are not fierce enough, the Hadith literature abounds with even greater imaginative horrors. Al-Bukhari 5:567 records that Muhammad said, "The least punished person of the hell-fire people on the Day of Resurrection will be a man under whose arch of the feet a smoldering ember will be placed so that his brain will boil because of it."

Needless to say, these ubiquitous and hair-raising images of hell serve to motivate Muslims to do all they can to avoid such a future. Muhammad is much in the tradition of John the Baptist and even Jesus at this point, for he functions truly as a warner of mortals concerning the horrible fate awaiting the wicked. His descriptions of hell find at least some of their antecedents in Jewish and Christian traditions stemming in part from New Testament teachings, where Jesus himself speaks of hell as a place of weeping and gnashing of teeth, a furnace of fire (Matt. 13:50) whose flames and punishments are everlasting (25:41), and a place of outer darkness (8:12) where the worm of decay never dies (Mark 9:48).

The book of Revelation pictures smoke and brimstone belching from the fires of hell (Rev. 9:2), fed ultimately by the great lake of fire (20:10). Perhaps the only significant difference between the biblical and Koranic accounts of hell is one of degree. The Koran portrays graphically and with great zest the agonies of the damned whereas the Bible remains relatively muted in its descriptions.

The Muslim Paradise of Sensual Pleasures

For Islam, paradise is the antithesis of hell.[4] In place of hell's physical agonies, paradise promises endless waves of sensual ecstasy. Hell consists of seven levels, but paradise contains eight (reflecting for some the hope that it will contain more inhabitants than the abode of the wicked). As with the Koranic names for hell, the names for paradise do not seem to indicate distinct levels, but many Islamic scholars nonetheless conceive them so. Generally, paradise in the Koran is expressed through the Arabic *al-Jannah* ("the Garden"). Our English word "paradise" comes through the Greek rendering (*paradeisos*) of an earlier Persian word (*al-Firdaus*), which found its way directly into Arabic and serves in the Koran as the name of one of the levels or descriptors of "the Garden." The eight levels of paradise depicted in the Koran are:

1. Garden of Eternity (25:15)
2. House of Peace (6:127)
3. House that Abides (40:39)
4. Gardens of Eden (9:72)
5. Gardens of Refuge (32:19)
6. Gardens of Delight (5:65)
7. ʿ*Illiyun* (also the name of the book of deeds of the righteous; 83:18–28)
8. Gardens of Paradise (*al-Firdaus*; 18:107).

Muslims, and only Muslims, will inhabit these various levels according to the merit of their lives and service.

Muhammad envisioned paradise as a place of almost boundless dimensions. According to al-Bukhari 8:559b, the prophet declared, "In Paradise there is a tree so big that a rider can travel in its shade for one hundred years without passing it." The rich and fertile land of the Garden is marked by multiple streams flowing variously with sweet water, milk, honey, or wine (Sura 47:15), from any of which the righteous are free to drink as much as they please. The blessed will dwell in cool gardens, recline on luxuriant couches, and wear beautiful garments.

The blessed will also be attended by eternally youthful boys, who serve them the widest array of fruits, delicacies, and goblets of fine wine. They will enjoy the sexual delights of the houris, who are a class of beautiful, young women specially created in paradise for the pleasure of the righteous (56:35–37). Fair in complexion, doe-eyed, and heretofore untouched by man or *jinni* (55:72–75), the houris are "spotless virgins, amorous, and of like age" (38:52) to the faithful Muslims of paradise. Their skin has the luster of fine jewels (56:22–23; 55:58), their breasts are of ample size (78:33), and they are eager to please. They will be married to the blessed men of paradise, apparently in addition to whatever wives remain from earthly days (44:54). These maidens will remain forever chaste and shy, with eyes only for their new husbands (37:48–49).

It seems fair to conclude that the Koranic emphasis on such sensual pleasures would appeal to a male follower of Muhammad from the seventh-century Arabian peninsula. Raised in an intensely hot, arid desert, forbidden the taste of wine, limited in sexual experience to his wife or wives, forced to eke out a living in a sparse, infertile land, what man would not salivate over the opportunity to recline on soft couches by endless streams of water, to be waited on to his heart's content by indefatigable servants bearing delicacies of fruits and meats, to enjoy free-flowing wine with never a hangover, to engage in sex with eternally virginal, voluptuous young women at his beck and call? Such a picture of paradise no doubt led many an Arab to throw in his lot with Muhammad.

To be fair to the prophet of Islam, the most sensual descriptions of paradise tend to be found in the earlier suras of his career, and in the later revelations he indicates that many of his followers will enter paradise as families and that believing men are to remain married to their earthly wives (though not to the exclusion of enjoying the houris). Nonetheless, sensual pleasures remain at the heart of paradise's allure.

Some modern Muslims counter that such graphic language in the Koran is meant to be understood metaphorically—an attempt to express in the limited language of human experience what is beyond our present conception. The exquisite spiritual pleasures of heaven find no real parallels on earth and so must be expressed in the language of pleasures we can understand. It is an injustice, they say, to take such language literally. However, Muslim religious leaders are surprisingly unified in their insistence that the Koran *is to be interpreted literally* concerning the sensual pleasures of paradise. Their perspective is summed up nicely in the words of one Arabian Muslim man:

> Today much effort is being spent to prove that Muhammad's paradise was only symbolic. Wise men explain away everything. But let me tell you this, I have lived my life faithful to God in this baking desert. I have avoided one earthly temptation after another in an effort to gain paradise. If I get there and find no cool rivers, no date trees and no beautiful girls . . . to keep me company, I shall feel badly defrauded.[5]

Little is said in the Koran or the Hadith traditions regarding the rewards available for faithful Muslim women. Presumably they too will enjoy the full range of culinary delights and will benefit from the service of the young attendants as they recline on couches in the same idyllic settings. But nothing is mentioned of them, and no provision is made for their sexual pleasure, except perhaps that they continue in conjugal relations with their earthly husband. For some, that seems less than paradisiacal!

The Stark Contrast with Heaven in the Bible

While Muslim and Christian understandings of hell differ principally in degree of description, the same cannot be said for their respective views on heaven or paradise. As we have noted, the Koran tantalizes the reader/listener with the sights, sounds, smells, tastes, and erotic feel of sensual delights. Paradise is the answer to a male hedonist's dreams.

God, however, is strangely absent from this dream. Paradise is essentially the contractual reward from Allah to the believer for sufficient obedience to his commands throughout one's earthly life or for sacrificing one's life in a *jihad* for him (this, by the way, was a strong ideological motivator behind the terrorist actions of 9/11, as the self-styled *mujahidin* gave up their lives convinced of the assurance that they would gain the pleasures of paradise). That reward is paid in terms of material blessings, some of which were strictly forbidden to Muslims on earth (e.g., sexual license and liberal use of wine) but are now encouraged in paradise.

Allah, who provides these pleasures, seems to hold himself apart from direct involvement with the righteous. His abode is not within paradise but above it. Even in the new creation, Allah remains so transcendent and "other" that it is difficult to conceive of him as communing with his creatures. Granted, a few Koranic verses speak of the blessed in paradise beholding God, but these isolated texts are lost among the many that trumpet the ecstasies of the flesh.

The contrast with the biblical view of heaven could not be more stark. While certain apocalyptic New Testament passages describe heaven in terms of jewels and precious metals, the intent of such images is clearly figurative. What matters most is the relationship of love that God promises to carry on with the redeemed, his adopted children. The heart of the biblical perspective on heaven may be found in Revelation 21–22, where John records his vision of the new heavens and the new earth:

> I saw the Holy City, the new Jerusalem, coming down out of heaven from God, prepared as a bride beautifully dressed for her husband. And I heard a loud voice from the throne saying, "Now the dwelling of God is with men, and he will live with them. They will be his people, and God himself will be with them and be their God. He will wipe every tear from their eyes. There will be no more death or mourning or crying or pain, for the old order of things has passed away." (Rev 21:2–4)

> No longer will there be any curse. The throne of God and of the Lamb will be in the city, and his servants will serve him. They will see his face, and his name will be on their foreheads. There will be no more night. They will not need the light of a lamp or the light of the sun, for the Lord God will give them light. And they will reign for ever and ever. (Rev. 22:3–5)

Here heaven is pictured primarily in terms of God's tender relationship with his people. He is the center of their attention, the fount and goal of every blessing. The joy of heaven is found not so much in pleasant circumstances as in the full experience of God's infinite love. All else pales in comparison to the fact that God chooses to dwell fully with his people, giving them his heart and receiving their adoration and love in return for endless ages.

If paradise for Muslims can be described as the ultimate trip to the most exquisite spa, heaven for Christians may be summarized as prodigals finally coming home to the secure embrace of our Father, the blessing of whose love knows no bounds. Fleshly pleasures may satisfy for a season, but only divine love can feed the human spirit for an eternity!

CHAPTER 10

What Is the Path of Jihad?

A young, self-assured gunslinger rides into Dodge City, looking for the resident ace. "This town ain't big enough for the two of us. Pack your bags or draw." So go the spaghetti Westerns. In the eyes of many, so goes the history of Islam during its first two centuries.

Recently, extensive terrorist activities by purportedly Muslim groups have increased debate over whether physical coercion is a normative part of Islam or not. Moderate Muslims say not, arguing that Islam is a religion of peace. In their minds, it is no more fair to judge Islam by extremists and political aberrations than it would be to tar and feather Christianity as a whole because of the Crusades, the Spanish Inquisition, and the Puritan witch hunts.

Is such a comparison fair? Does it do justice to the canonical teachings of both religions? The answer to these questions is found at least partly in a study of the Islamic concept of *jihad* and its lack of a full counterpart in the writings of the New Testament and Christian orthodoxy.

Jihad of Mouth, Pen, and Hand

The word *jihad* is often translated as "holy war," but literally means "struggle, exertion." The phrase "holy war" never occurs in the Koran, but it does serve as a catchall term under which are gathered a number of Arabic words found in the Koran.

ARABIC TERM IN KORAN	TIMES IN KORAN	MEANING OF THE TERM
qital	33 times	Fighting with a weapon so as to kill or subdue
harb	6 times	Military attack or war against unbelievers
jihad	28 times	A fight against evil taking many forms: heart, mouth, pen, hand, and sword

All Muslims are called to engage in *jihad* of the heart, which finds a rough parallel in the Christian teaching to put to death the sinful nature. Muhammad clearly commands commitment to struggle against one's own sinful tendencies, though this is not aided by a new nature resident in the heart through the Holy Spirit, as in Christian understanding. *Jihad* of heart, mouth, and pen are sometimes spoken of as "spiritual *jihad*," particularly among the Shi'ites (the largest minority party of Islam, comprising roughly 10 percent of the Muslim world).

"*Jihad* of the mouth" is understood in two related ways. Its goal is to undermine opposition to Islam by means of speech, either in the form of verbal argumentation (finding a Christian parallel in the practice of apologetics) or that of curses and saber-rattling. The latter finds its roots in pre-Islamic Arabia, where the art of extemporaneous imprecatory poetry was prized as a means of verbal jousting between warring tribes. A war of words was usually considered preferable to one of physical violence.

This approach continues in the Muslim world today. When Saddam Hussein bragged before the first Gulf War that coalition troops were facing "the mother of all battles" and would endure crushing defeat, he was engaging in a *jihad* of the mouth. Similarly, the Taliban leadership of Afghanistan vowed repeatedly in the fall of 2001 that U.S. forces would never topple their government but would turn tail and run in ignominious defeat, as the Soviets had over a decade before.

"*Jihad* of the pen" utilizes the written word for the same end. Over the last thirteen centuries, much Islamic ink has been employed to present Muhammad as the perfect man and ultimate prophet of God and his message as the perfect will of Allah for all humanity. The central doctrines of the Christian faith, though sadly misunderstood by many Muslim scholars, have been the special target of Islamic apologetic works.

"*Jihad* of the hand" seeks to promote the cause of Allah against evil by accomplishing praiseworthy deeds. The good example of Muslims in their treatment of others and devotion to God serves as a witness to the superiority of their message and as a vehicle for the proclamation of their beliefs. Parallels with Christianity here are clear. Saint Francis of Assisi, for example, is credited with saying, "Preach the gospel at all times; if necessary, use words."

Jihad of the Sword

The last and most troublesome form of *jihad* is the "*jihad* of the sword." That this has been the primary understanding of *jihad* in Islamic history and jurisprudence is beyond doubt. When the word *jihad* occurs in the Koran without any modifier or with the typical modifier "in the cause of Allah," it invariably refers to armed combat on behalf of Islam. It is often linked with the word *qital* in the context of dealing with unbelievers.

Some modern Muslims downplay this understanding, arguing that in Islamic tradition such violence is called the "lesser *jihad*." Indeed, this is true. According to one disputed Hadith tradition, when the messenger of Allah (Muhammad) returned from the field of war, he said, "We have all returned from the lesser *jihad* to the greater *jihad*." Some companions asked, "What is the greater *jihad*, O prophet of God?" He replied, "*Jihad* against the desires." Presumably the *jihad* of the heart is greater because it is unceasing, whereas the *jihad* of the sword continues only as long as there are unbelievers unwilling to submit to the rule of Islam.

Nonetheless, this tradition demonstrates that Muhammad himself was engaged regularly in military *jihad* and commanded his followers to engage in it as well. Sources from the Koran, the Hadith, and the early Islamic biographies of Muhammad place the Arabian prophet actively in seventy military attacks or battles. Several times the Koran declares that the armed conflicts led by Muhammad were predestined by Allah to occur, having already been recorded in the books of heaven. Twelve times Muslims are commanded explicitly to engage in *qital*, six times to commit themselves to *jihad* in the way of Allah.

The Enemies of Islam

The Koran speaks often of the enemies of Islam. Though generally they may be described as any who refuse to embrace the message of Muhammad, more specifically the Koran categorizes them in one of three ways. The *kufar* (unbelievers) are those who disbelieve Muhammad's message, particularly as revealed in the six central articles of faith propounded by Islam: belief in the sovereign uniqueness of Allah, in angels, in all Allah's messengers, in his revealed holy books, in the Day of Judgment, and in divine predestination. Those who die in a state of *kufr* (unbelief) will be consigned to hell. Those unbelievers who oppose the spread of Islam must be defeated by whatever means necessary.

The *mushrikun* are those who engage in the sin of *shirk*, linking anything in the created order with Allah as his equal. Hence all polytheists and idolaters fall into this category. Interestingly, the Koran also declares all Jews and Christians who do not accept Islam to be *mushrikun* and thus enemies of the true faith. According to 5:82, the Jews in particular are among those with the strongest hatred toward Muslims, whereas Christians in general are described as "nearest in love to the believers" (i.e., Muslims). Nonetheless, Muslims are specifically commanded not to befriend Christians, Jews, or other non-Muslims (3:28; 4:89; 5:51).

The final enemy of Islam forms the category of the hypocrites. These are former or lapsed Muslims, who renege on their faith commitment publicly, who turn to another faith and thus become traitors to Allah and his prophet, or who by their public lifestyle demonstrate clear hypocrisy to what they profess with their lips. In these ways they bring harm to the *ummah* (Muslim community) and become objects of a triple curse from Allah, the angels, and all humankind (2:161; 3:86–87). Although the Koran does not decree their execution, Sharia law does (the system of national laws derived from the Koran and traditions of Muhammad). In many Muslim communities it is a matter of family honor to compel such individuals to return to the Islamic fold or, failing this, to kill them. In terms of eternity, the fate of such hypocrites is to roast in the deepest fires of hell.

Four Stages in Muhammad's Teaching

Thus, the Koran prescribes *jihad* against Islam's enemies. Yet for those unfamiliar with the Koran, much confusion results from a study of passages dealing with *jihad* of the sword, because there seem to be contradictory teachings. Islamic scholars, however, note that Muhammad's teaching on *jihad* developed over time as the circumstances of his early community changed, which accounts for these contradictions. Four distinct stages are evident.

1. Peaceful Persuasion

When Islam was a fledgling movement and Muhammad endured increasing persecution from his extended tribe in Mecca for preaching absolute monotheism, he counseled his small band to engage in a policy of peaceful persuasion and ready pardon of unbelievers for transgressions. Sura 16:125–6 declares: "Invite [all] to the way of thy Lord with wisdom and beautiful preaching; and argue with them in ways that are best and most gracious. . . . But if you show patience, that is indeed the best [course] for those who are patient." Many Muslims today regard this as the proper approach for the Muslim community any time it finds itself the overwhelming minority in an unreceptive host culture.

2. Warding Off Aggression

When Muhammad fled Mecca in 622 to the friendlier confines of Medina (a migration known as the *Hijrah*; see chapter 2), the movement grew significantly. His followers back in Mecca began to face serious persecution in the loss of property and threat of bodily harm. In large part this resistance was a response to the Prophet's continuing attacks on the Meccan caravan trade—the primary means by which Muhammad financed his mission and community. Muhammad subsequently decreed that fighting was permissible only to ward off aggression and reclaim goods and property confiscated by infidels. So, for example, Sura 22:39 says:

> To those against whom war is made, permission is given [to fight], because they are wronged, and verily, God is most powerful for their aid. [They are] those who have been expelled from their homes in defiance of right, [for no cause] except that they say, "Our Lord is God."

Within a few months, this permission to fight in self-defense was made a religious obligation. Believers were to engage in warfare against those who initiated hostilities against the Muslim community or its interests.

> Fight in the cause of God those who fight you, but do not transgress limits; for God loveth not transgressors. And slay them wherever you catch them, and turn them out from where they have turned you out.... But if they fight you, slay them. Such is the reward of those who suppress faith. (2:190–94)

Notice that at this point Muhammad shows great concern that such fighting remain within strictly prescribed limits. *Jihad* was not to give license to indiscriminate violence in the name of Allah.

3. From Defensive to Offensive

As the doctrine of *jihad* developed, Muhammad taught that those who sacrificed their lives in battle for the cause of God would be guar-

anteed admission to the highest level of heaven—no small reward in
a religion where one's hope of heaven otherwise depends on one's near-
perfect obedience to divine law. Conversely, those able-bodied Muslims who refused the summons would suffer divine punishment (9:38–
39). Moreover, Muhammad decreed that all booty collected in conquest should be distributed among the *mujahidin* (those engaged in
jihad). Nine verses in the Koran speak specifically of booty and how it
is properly distributed. Another thirty verses deal with the treatment
of slaves (those taken prisoner) now owned by Muslims as a result of
the division of booty from successful battles. Not surprisingly, the
number of Muslim men willing to commit their lives to holy war
surged from this point on.[1]

This third stage of development moved *jihad* from defensive in
nature to offensive. Muslims were now to take the initiative in war, but
they were to refrain from attacks during the four sacred months (recognized by all tribes within the Arabian peninsula as months for pilgrimage to various religious shrines at Mecca and elsewhere). "When
the forbidden months are past, then fight and slay the pagans wherever
you find them, and seize them, beleaguer them, and lie in wait for them
in each and every ambush. But if they repent, perform the prayers and
give alms, then leave their way free" (9:5).

4. Expansionist *Jihad*

The final development of the Koranic concept of *jihad* removed
any limitations on when fighting in the cause of Allah could be initiated. When commanded by a recognized Muslim leader, military attack
against non-Muslims was deemed appropriate in any season and on any
land not yet surrendered to the armies of Islam.

> Fight those who believe not in God nor the last day, nor hold
> to be forbidden that which has been forbidden by God and
> His Apostle, nor acknowledge the religion of truth, [even if they
> are] of the people of the Book [i.e., Jews and Christians], until
> they pay the jizya (an often humiliating poll-tax exacted from

conquered non-Muslims) with willing submission and feel themselves subdued. (9:29)

Which of these stages is meant to be normative for Islam? According to standard Islamic jurisprudence, it is the fourth (i.e., expansionist *jihad*), understood as armed struggle against unbelievers, whether or not the Muslim community has been attacked. According to the law of abrogation in Koranic hermeneutics (see Suras 2:106; 13:39; 16:103), when there is a conflict of or change in teaching, later revelation always trumps earlier texts.

Hence, the primary definition of *jihad* will always entail the obligation to offer one's material resources in the cause of Allah and strive militarily, if need be, against the unbelieving world until it surrenders willingly to the rule of Allah as expressed religio-politically in Sharia law. *Jihad* is a duty incumbent on the international Muslim community as long as there remains any resistance to universal Islamic rule. Hence, in Islamic circles, the timeline of *jihad* is framed in maxims such as "until the Day of Resurrection" or "until the end of the world."

At the Time of Muhammad's Death

Expansionist *jihad* was clearly the understanding of the Muslim community at the time of Muhammad's death. In one century's time from the appointment of the first caliph, Abu Bakr, the reach of Islam extended from a limited religion of the Arabian peninsula to an empire reaching across North Africa up to Spain in the west, and across Asia into India in the east. Muslim armies swept through the remnants of the Byzantine and Sassanid realms, often encountering little outright resistance but fighting where necessary. By the end of the second century A.H. (*Anno Hijrah*), Muslim territorial conquests had peaked, and Islamic jurisprudence had fully defined the proper behaviors and conditions governing "holy war." These laws, now comprising part of Sharia, were developed by Muslim jurists from their study of the Koran and of the "inspired" practices of Muhammad (as related in the Hadith and authoritative biographies).

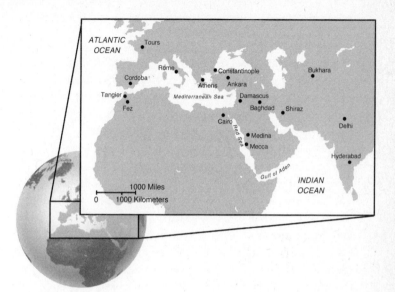

The whole of Sharia law comprises two major sections: one dealing with divine-human regulations and the other with human interrelationships. Each of these sections is further divided into two categories: laws dealing with personal, individual behaviors and concerns, and laws involving communal, public issues (criminal law). The body of law dealing with *jihad* falls into this latter category.

The importance of this subject for early Islam is demonstrated by the fact that in the development of these laws concerning *jihad*, ninety-five different Koranic texts are considered and cited. This number dwarfs by comparison the number of verses considered in the formation of laws for any of the other areas (e.g., prayer, marriage, inheritance, etc.). There can be no doubt that for the nascent Muslim community, "holy war" (as defined by the terms *jihad* and *qital*) was understood primarily as a call to armed conflict, and it was regulated by laws to ensure its legitimacy according to the Koran and recognized traditions.

Contrasting Responses of Two Religions

Not surprisingly, perhaps, these defining laws closely parallel Augustine's "just war" conditions in the Western Christian tradition. *Jihad* is only to be conducted under the proper governmental authorization; it must avoid harm to noncombatants, hostages, prisoners, and property (especially trees and landscape), and its ultimate goal must be to secure justice and peace. For Islam, however, the causes of justice and peace are synonymous with the advance of the Muslim state, for politics and spirituality are inextricably bound together in the dream of one world under the complete reign of Allah and his followers. Thus, whereas "just war" principles do not in theory support the notion of establishing the kingdom of God by force, the Islamic doctrine of *jihad* unapologetically does so.

That this is true can be seen from the disparate responses of the two religions to the record of violence for political ends in their respective historical traditions. When the church has looked back on its dalliances with coercive power reflected in the Crusades, the Inquisition, and the like, its response is generally one of shame and repentance, for the teachings of Jesus eschew force as a means of accomplishing God's will on earth. When the church loses its focus on the fact that the kingdom of God is established by divine agency and not by human power, that Jesus declared his kingdom is not "of this world," that "those who live by the sword will die by the sword," that the terms of conquest employed by Jesus were self-sacrificing love and not the application of military, economic, or social power, that is when it has turned to the methods of the world around it, with disastrous consequences.

By contrast, when the *ummah* of Islam faces its history of coercion and expansion, there is no corresponding shame or repentance, for Islam teaches in its most authoritative sources that force is justifiable in the cause of Allah. Indeed, many Muslims look back on the first three centuries of Islam as the golden years of their heritage and long for a return to world ascendancy. Far from feeling regret over past conquests, Islam takes pride in this heritage.

Explaining Old Testament Violence

Critics of Christianity point out that the Old Testament historical books portray God as commanding Israel to military violence that was every bit as bloody as anything in the Koran. True enough. But there are some vital differences to consider. (1) The commands are framed in terms of divine judgment on the pagan nations inhabiting the Promised Land. Israel is to drive out these nations not only to possess the land herself but as an expression of the holiness of God. She is further warned that if she fails to obey God, she too will be driven from the land.

(2) Once in Canaan, Israel was never commanded to engage in the systematic conquest of the rest of the world. Rather, she is called through her life with God to act as a light to the nations, who through her holy example should be drawn to the worship of the one true God.

(3) The history of Israel as a political nation has limited application to the purpose of the church in the world today. The primary battle of the church is summed up in Ephesians 6:10–18, reminding us that our fight is not against flesh and blood but rather against the spiritual powers of darkness. Compare the first three centuries of Christian expansion with the first three centuries of Islamic expansion, and you will quickly see the empirical difference between how the two faiths propagated themselves—Islam, in large measure by the threat or exercise of force; Christianity, by peaceful proclamation and the example of love.

The Contrasting View of Muhammad and Jesus

Two closing illustrations will show the stark contrast of perspective between the founders of each religion in question. When Jesus was arrested at the Garden of Gethsemane, the disciples grabbed their swords. Peter actually unsheathed his and struck off the ear of one opponent. Jesus immediately commanded his followers to calm down and declared that violence is not the appropriate means to accomplish his Father's will. According to Matthew 26:53, Jesus claimed that if he wanted to win a military victory, all he needed do was call on his Father, "who will at once put at my disposal more than twelve legions of angels." But he did not. Instead, rebellion was met with love, animosity with forgiveness.

Moreover, while hanging on the cross, Jesus prayed to his Father on behalf of those who had shown themselves to be enemies, "Father, forgive them, for they know not what they are doing" (Luke 23:34). Love for enemies, sacrifice for their reconciliation to God, is the way of Jesus.

According Sahih al-Bukhari (4:280b), one of several oft-repeated stories about Muhammad reads thus:

> Anas bin Malik said, "Allah's Apostle entered (Mecca) in the year of the conquest (of Mecca) wearing a helmet over his head." After he took it off, a man came and said, "Ibn Khatal [a pagan opponent] is clinging to the curtains of the Ka'aba [a recognized behavior for seeking mercy]." The Prophet said, "Kill him."

While there is certainly room for debate over how well throughout history Christians and Muslims have followed the teaching of their respective leaders, there is no doubt over the contrasting visions of Jesus and Muhammad as to how the kingdom of God should be advanced on earth. So, while the Augustinian just war theory has played a relatively minor role in the spread of Christianity across the globe, *jihad* has been at the heart of Islam's expansion.

Militancy or Moderation?

Today perhaps more than ever, Islam worldwide faces a trenchant, internal struggle between fundamentalist militancy on the one hand, which reads the Koran literalistically (and has amassed huge amounts of tradition to support its viewpoints), and moderate Islam on the other, which seeks to spread the faith irenically or simply to live inconspicuously in multicultural settings. The militant approach has been behind the majority of regional conflicts in the last few decades, which ironically have erupted principally in Muslim-dominated lands and have been cast by one side or the other as a *jihad* against enemies of the faith.

Whether this trend continues or not will depend ultimately on who wins the hearts of the masses with the more compelling picture of

Islam—the moderates with their desire for peaceful coexistence and the betterment of humanity through moral reformation and the peaceful propagation of Islam, or the militant Muslims with their cry for a return to the ways of early Islam and the use of force against all who refuse to submit to their strict, but traditional, vision. The world awaits the results of this struggle with bated breath, worried about the possibility of future cataclysms.

The Call to Peacemaking

In the midst of all this, the church of Jesus Christ is called to the role of peacemaking, of reaching out in genuine love to all, but especially now to the Muslim world. Jesus commands us to love Muslims as our neighbors, seeking their best interests as we seek our own. While we cannot decide for the Islamic world which path it will choose, we can choose our own path, the way of the cross, the lifestyle that is willing to give itself away for the welfare of others, even those who call us "enemy." Such was the way of Jesus. Such must be the way of his people.

Epilogue: The Risk of Ignorance

Why devote an entire book to the Koran? Isn't this a subject of interest only to Muslims and scholars of religion? Not at all. As Islam, the religion of the Koran, continues to advance across the world, the need grows for greater understanding of the Muslim holy book. There are great risks in ignoring the religion and revelation of Muhammad—the risks of apathy, of misunderstanding, sinful stereotyping, or naïve acceptance on the one hand, and the risk of thoughtless demonizing on the other. These risks only grow as Muslims increasingly intermingle among the population of today's America.

Last week a woman I'd never met called to ask my advice on a Bible to purchase for a young Muslim friend. He was a dating a Christian girl and wanted to learn more about Christianity. Yesterday after our Sunday worship service, a recent college graduate shared with me about a close female friend of hers who will be married next year in Pakistan in a traditional Muslim wedding. My parishioner, wishing to avoid any possible cultural or religious offense, wanted to know what kind of gift might be appropriate in celebration of this engagement news.

Twenty years ago, questions like these would have been rare in my life. Now they are regular occurrences, not because I have developed a higher profile but because the waves of Islamic life are lapping increasingly at the shores of the American church. Most Americans still know little about Islam, and often what they think they know has been shaped more by caricature than by fact. Certainly after the fanatical terrorist strikes of September 11, 2001, many in the West are skittish over having any dealings with Muslims or those who "look Islamic," whatever that may mean to the untrained eye.

Where there is ignorance, there is often fear, even though the vast majority of Muslims in America are interested in being good neighbors, enjoying the freedoms our Constitution provides, and being helpful contributors to American society. Many Americans unfortunately equate being Arab or Muslim with an inclination toward violence and terrorism, and they are deeply concerned about the growth of Islam and the teaching of the Koran in the United States and the spread of ideas that come out of the Koran.

Pepsi or Coke?

Many Christians are concerned for an entirely different reason. Hearing reports that Islam may be the fastest growing religion in this country (in terms of percentage growth, that is, not in terms of gross numbers), followers of Christ rue the fact that increasing numbers of people are turning to Islam rather than to Christ for their security in life and death. To the outsider with no religious convictions, this may seem like a petty squabble over market share, much like Pepsi and Coke vying for bragging rights over a new generation of consumers. However, for Muslims and Christians alike the stakes appear infinitely higher.

Both movements have the mandate of their founder to reach the world with their message. Of all the major world religions, these two are far and away the most mission-minded. Further, each is exclusivistic when it comes to the matter of salvation, teaching that the way hearers respond to its message alone will determine their destinies in heaven or hell. Both Islam and Christianity believe that the hope of the world is tied exclusively to their respective, yet contradictory plans of salvation, so that to believe one religion is necessarily to reject the other. For this crucial reason, Christianity and Islam can never be mere competitors, like Coke and Pepsi, but rather remain rivals on a cosmic scale, for the stakes are of eternal consequence. Because there can be no compromise on such issues of ultimate importance, the two faiths will always remain adversarial with regard to their goals.

As Christians consider the relatively fast rise of Islam in the West, then, there is cause for apprehension. Two questions clamor to be answered:

- What is the cause of such rapid increase in Islam's numbers in our midst?
- How ought the church (and individual Christians) respond to the challenge of a growing Muslim community around us?

Reasons for the Growth of Islam

I should begin by stating that much of the recent growth of Islam in the West is due to two sociological realities. Muslims account for a large percentage of immigrants coming from Africa, the Middle East, and Asia, and so swell the numbers of Muslims in the West—not by conversion but by resettlement. Second, non-Western Muslim couples tend to bear significantly more children than found in the average Western family, and so some notable numerical increase is due to a more vigorous birthrate. Having recognized these important realities, however, it nonetheless remains true that Islam is also growing through conversion of non-Muslims to Islam. In our own American context, the reasons for this are at least fivefold.

(1) Primary among them is the spiritual vacuum pervading our culture. As the church over the last two centuries has gradually lost its own moorings and drifted away from influence on American society, our culture has increasingly lost its spiritual and moral weightiness. Although many contenders have sought to fill the gap left by a receding, ineffec-

tual church, none of them has had the kind of substance to challenge the place of the gospel in American life until the arrival of Islam on our shores. As Christian denominations have squabbled over relatively petty issues, divided over traditional moral absolutes, and substituted a non-descript ethic of tolerance for the strong meat of the gospel, Islam has stormed into the public arena with a clear, self-confident worldview and a message from the Koran unhampered by cultural compromise.

(2) To many Americans the preaching of the church seems tired and trite, having been drained of life through the multiplication of clichés and dull repetition of uninspired catch phrases. Islam, by con-trast, comes with a language new to American ears and thus sounds fresh and alive to the jaded post-Christian listener. Even though most of Islam's core ethical and spiritual teachings are found in Christianity, they appear clothed in new raiment and come across as attractive and different. Teachings that elicit a yawn when spoken by a preacher evoke excitement when proclaimed by an imam. Truth, after all, remains truth. What has changed is the willingness to lend an ear to something that appears new and mysterious to an uninformed Western audience.

(3) Islam without apology makes radical demands on its followers. Those who submit to its claims often undergo seismic shifts in their beliefs and lifestyles. Many people are attracted to a religion that demands ultimate allegiance—something worth dying for. And, of course, something worth dying for is also worth living for.

Certainly this call to ultimate allegiance also characterizes biblical Christianity. Jesus himself said, "If anyone would come after me, he must deny himself and take up his cross and follow me. For whoever wants to save his life will lose it, but whoever loses his life for me will find it" (Matt. 16:24–25; see also 10:37). Paul, the great apostolic mis-sionary, wrote what might aptly be called his life motto in Philippians 1:21, "For me to live is Christ and to die is gain." But how often do we see such passion and commitment in the Western church today? All too often the gospel we embrace has been domesticated and gelded. It is to be petted and admired but rarely let out of its cage.

The bold claims of Christ on our lives have been enfeebled to such a point that to be a Christian in many of our churches seems to require little or nothing in belief or action to distinguish us from a well-off secular humanist. Outsiders looking at the church find few positive distinctives separating the Christian subculture from the larger culture of American life. Not surprisingly, then, when spiritually hungry seekers find Muslims committed to pursuing a countercultural lifestyle with a higher standard than the cultural norm, they are often impressed and attracted.

(4) Islam is also unapologetically directive as to the do's and don'ts in life. Surrounded by a sea of gray, the moral certitude of Islam's commandments stand out starkly in black and white. Thus, in a postmodern, ethically relative age where many feel uncomfortably adrift morally and yearn for an authority to tell them how to act, Islam provides a haven in which to anchor themselves. The believer is not required to understand how all the commands and taboos fit together into a comprehensive worldview, only to obey what Islamic scholarship has laid down in Sharia law as interpreted by an imam or court.

(5) Islam has in the last half of the twentieth century recaptured the early faith's vision of conquering the world in the name of Allah. After a relative hibernation on the heels of the collapse of the Ottoman Empire in 1924, Islamic groups are once again enthusiastically moving outward into the world and now extending their influence into heretofore relatively unreached territories, including Europe and the United States. Renewed by missionary zeal, many Muslims are propagating their beliefs and practices with deep conviction that is rarely matched by other groups, including most American Christians.

A Foothold in the African-American Community

For these reasons at least, the religion of the Koran is becoming a formidable player on the American religious scene. In particular, it has gained a strong foothold in the African-American community. While the reasons for this are no doubt complex and beyond the scope of this epilogue, several observations may be made with some degree of confidence.

(1) The American church has all too often failed to make crystal clear by its proclamation and lifestyle that the gospel of Jesus Christ is good news for people of *all races, ethnic groups, and social standings*. As the apostle Paul declares, because of God's work of salvation in Christ, there is now no longer Jew nor Greek, slave nor free, male nor female (and we might add, black or white, rich or poor), for all are one in Christ Jesus (Gal. 3:28). The sinful stain of racism in the church has certainly contributed to the African-American community looking elsewhere for a spiritual home. For many, Christianity is identified with "white America" and with the hateful institution of slavery in our country, dating back to colonial days. These individuals rightly or wrongly have written off Christianity, yet they remain hungry for spiritual sustenance. Islam purports to meet this need, and many turn to it with fervent hope.

(2) Other African Americans in their search for identity look back to their African roots and reason that since Islam must have been the religion of their ancestors, it should be theirs also. Though this logic is highly dubious (it is at least as likely that their ancestors were Christian or animist, since both these religious orientations predated Islam on the African continent), it nonetheless serves a sociological purpose in enabling African Americans to feel they are connecting with their roots and establishing a unique identity separate from but equal to, if not greater than, that of the "white Christian establishment."

Such a racial approach to religious affiliation seems to hold particularly great attraction for African Americans incarcerated in federal and state prisons, where loyalty to one's own race over against other groups is deemed essential. One marker of this loyalty is the adoption of Islam as "the black man's religion" in contrast to white supremacists or born-again Christians.

The danger of misusing Islam as the native religion of any one race (which orthodox Islam itself eschews) is that such a mindset easily degenerates into religious racism. One finds identity not so much in Islam itself as in being black and having one's unique religion not open to those of other races (in this case, particularly whites). The Black Muslim movement, which gathered steam in the tumultuous 1960s and continues to play itself out today under the charismatic leadership of Louis Farrakhan, is a sad testament to such perspectives.

In fairness to Islam, orthodox Muslims have always repudiated the Black Muslim movement, which claimed its leader, Elijah Muhammad, to be a true prophet whose teachings supplanted all those who preceded him, including the Arabian prophet Muhammad. In recent decades, Elijah Muhammad's son has moved his followers away from the heresy of his father and led the bulk of them into the orthodox fold. However, he has found it difficult to make this transition stick among his African-American adherents, and recently he retired from his leadership role in frustration over the sluggish response of the leaders under his charge to embrace mainstream Islam. The future of this movement remains very much an open question, but it cannot be gainsaid that Islam finds a strongly receptive audience in the African-American subculture.

A Challenge to Today's Church

In many ways, the relative success of Islam in our midst should serve as a rebuke to the church of Jesus Christ for our poor witness to the grace and truth of our Lord. For the sake of Muslims and all others who are hungry to connect with a personal god, we Christians must make sure that the dividing walls of human hostility that Christ destroyed at the cross are not rebuilt through our own sins of racism or apathy. We must embrace fully and act on the truth that distinctions of skin color or ethnic background have no place in the body of Christ; all people are equally and warmly welcomed into God's kingdom as they come in repentance and trust in Jesus Christ. We must stand clearly and unequivocally for the foundational truths of the Christian faith and, as disciples of our Lord, put into practice the ethical standards of the gospel.[1]

We must own the truth that Christianity and Islam will always remain opponents—and likely in increasing measure as this twenty-first century unfolds. Therefore, Christians need to become much more familiar with the teachings of the Koran and the practices of Islam so as to more ably explain to Muslims the reason for the hope that lies within us because of Jesus Christ. The important field of apologetics has been focused almost exclusively on the challenges of modernism (and, more recently, postmodernism). We need to restock our intellectual tool shed, laying aside the tools of Enlightenment debate and crafting new ones that will help open the Muslim mind and heart to the matchless excellencies of Jesus Christ.

We must become active ambassadors of Christ's love, even toward those who declare themselves sworn enemies of the cross. Though some in the Muslim world may call for *jihad* against all infidels, we are to act according to the mandate of our Master and so to love Muslims along with all other neighbors. The famous Johannine passage "God so loved the world . . ." includes Muslims in God's love as much as anyone else.

We must rest our confidence in the sovereign work of God. The present influx of Muslim immigrants provides the American church with wonderful opportunities for reaching people whom fifty years ago we would never have dreamed of meeting. Instead of responding with fear, we should find joy and excitement in the fact that God has brought the mission field into our backyard (in some cases literally!).

Since God has already won the day against sin, death, and the devil at the cross of Christ, we can rest confident in the knowledge that his plans and purposes are unassailable. According to his sovereign will and design, the gospel will ultimately prevail. Our responsibility is to pray for the renewal of the church, for our own renewal, and for the responsiveness of the world around us, that God will use us in love and power to effectively reach the world for Christ. Then we are to step forward in faith.

Falling in Love Again

Yet for all the above imperatives to really happen, for the church to become truly effective as a missionary body to the Muslim world, one thing above all else is paramount and precedes all other priorities. We, the bride of Christ, must fall in love again with our Bridegroom. We must live with a passion that never tires of singing his praises and enjoying his presence. We must be awed once again by the dimensions of his boundless grace, the length and width and height and depth of his sacrificial love, the unrelenting nature of his heart, which pursues rebels—not to execute them as they deserve but to win them to his kingdom and shower them with undeserved gifts.

It is only when we have discovered once again our first love and find ourselves intoxicated with Christ that we will have something compelling to say to the Muslim world, something powerful enough to free them from slavery to the written word of the Koran to the liberty of the living Spirit of God. Then, I believe with my whole being, when we speak from a heart captivated by Christ, the Muslim world will sit up and take notice—indeed, not only the Muslim world, but with them Hindus, Buddhists, Taoists, agnostics, and atheists, people from every tribe and tongue and land and nation—for then will Jesus Christ, God the Son, be glorified worthily as Lord and Savior, together with God the Father and God the Holy Spirit, one holy, triune God, from whom flows all true love. Only then, I believe, will we begin to see fulfilled the words of the prophet Isaiah:

> In that day there will be a highway from Egypt to Assyria. The Assyrians will go to Egypt and the Egyptians to Assyria. The Egyptians and Assyrians will worship together. In that day Israel will be the third, along with Egypt and Assyria, a blessing on the earth. The LORD Almighty will bless them, saying, "Blessed be Egypt my people, Assyria my handiwork, and Israel my inheritance." (Isa. 19:23–25)

May the Lord Jesus bring this to pass in our day.

CHAPTER 1:
The Koran through Muslim Eyes

1. The author describes in some detail how reverently Muslims treat copies of the Koran. Do you think this is a positive thing or smacks of bibliolatry (excessive reverence for the Bible)? Compare and discuss such treatment with how many Christians typically treat copies of the Bible. If you note major differences, why do you think that is so?

2. Learning the Koran figures dominantly in the typical school program in the Arab world. What are some of the implications of living in a culture where religious training is compulsory versus our own, where it is not?

3. Like Christians, Muslims place a high value on reading Scripture and memorizing it. How might such knowledge influence your interactions with someone of the Muslim faith?

4. As the author notes, religious people of all stripes desire to know and carry out God's will but often resort to superstitions to fulfill their hunger. What do you make of this, and again, how might you use such knowledge in conversations with a Muslim?

5. Using examples from the chapter, discuss some of the ways Islam seems to be a religion of rule-keeping. Considering Jesus' teaching in the Gospels, especially in his confrontations with the Pharisees (see, e.g., Matt. 12:1–12; 15:1–9), contrast Christianity and Islam.

6. The author closes the chapter by contrasting Islamic worship and Christian worship. What are some of these differences and how might they affect an individual's view of God and attitudes about life?

CHAPTER 2:
Where Did the Koran Come From?

1. The author writes, "The Koran and Muhammad have a symbiotic relationship. It is all but impossible to discuss the one without in some way including the other." Would you agree that a similar relationship exists between the Bible and Jesus Christ? Why or why not?

2. Using biographical information provided by the author, compare and contrast the life of Muhammad and the life of Christ. Also, discuss the idea that one claimed to *bring* the word of God (Allah) and the other claimed to *be* the Word made flesh. Would you compare Muhammad more with someone like Moses or Paul or with Christ? Why?

3. Muslims and Christians both hold to their Scriptures being divinely inspired, yet both cannot be accepted as ultimately true since they point in vastly different directions. How do you personally deal with these conflicting truth claims, especially in conversations with Muslim friends or acquaintances? (Contrast the fact that Muhammad occasionally corrected or revised passages in the Koran with the Christian teaching that the Bible is infallible, i.e., incapable of error.)

4. As the author points out, Muhammad developed an unyielding commitment to monotheism in a highly polytheistic culture. What circumstances do you think may have contributed to his belief? How might Islam's adherence to monotheism be a positive when witnessing to a Muslim? How might it be a negative?

5. Muslims argue that the Koran's literary beauty proves its divine nature and therefore its truth, yet the author argues otherwise. Discuss the two arguments and your own personal observations. What are some other Bible passages besides the one referenced ("Satan himself masquerades as an angel of light," see 2 Cor. 11:14) that support the author's view?

6. Muhammad countered religious critics of his day, who argued that true prophets performed miracles, that the Koran was his one miracle. Imagine for a moment you are Muhammad and make your defense, then "switch sides" and present his opponents' point of view. What are the "signs" of a Christian prophet or apostle?

CHAPTER 3:
And the Word Became . . . Paper?

1. How significant do you think it is that prior to the Koran the Arab people had no Scripture in their own tongue? What does that tell us about humankind in general? About their desire for spirituality?

2. The author offers extended historical background to demonstrate that the Koran did not exist as an undisputed, uniform text from the beginning. Why is this important in understanding Islam and its (as well as Muhammad's) reliability?

3. If a "discovery" was unearthed that apparently undermined the reliability of the Bible, do you think you would be able to hold firmly to your faith, or would you waver? How do you deal with seeming discrepancies within the biblical text or with attacks on the Bible by scholarly critics? What, if any, are your own questions about the inspiration and writing of the Christian Scriptures?

4. Uthman, one of Muhammad's successors, valued political unity above theological integrity. His standardization of the Koran has become the adopted text for thirteen centuries since. What are the consequences when human wisdom and desires replace God's—in any religion?

5. Despite the seeming fact that the Koran does not exist in an unaltered form, the author urges Christians not to show Muslims disrespect by attacking their Scriptures. He advises instead to focus on a relationship (with Jesus, the Living Word) instead of on a book. What are some practical ways you might do this in your interactions with those of the Muslim faith?

6. Speaking of Scripture in unaltered form, how do you think the Bible in its many translations and paraphrases fits into this discussion? How would you respond to a Muslim who questioned you about the reliability of or need for these many versions?

CHAPTER 4:
Will the Real Jesus Please Stand Up?

1. Respond to the words of Omar (see page 54) that begin with the statement, "We Muslims have a higher view of Jesus than many Christians I know." Discuss the mixed messages that Muslims hear about Christ and how these messages might be a stumbling block for them in accepting the gospel.

2. Compare and contrast the Koran's and the Bible's view of Mary. How does the Koran's depiction of Mary coincide with the Islamic attitude toward women in much of the world today?

3. Although Muslims have no problem accepting Jesus' virgin birth or his many miracles, they reject out of hand his divinity and the

doctrine of the Trinity. Using the information from the chapter, discuss not only what Muhammad "got right" but why you think he stopped short of believing some of the most critical teachings about Jesus.

4. According to Muhammad, Jesus was simply one from a long line of prophets with the same message as all the rest (i.e., he brought no new revelation). How does that teaching conflict with Jesus' own teaching about himself (see, e.g., John 14:6)?

5. The Koran denies two central doctrines of the Christian Scriptures: the need for a Savior (our inability to absolve our own sin) and Jesus' sacrificial death on the cross. How do these particular beliefs affect how a Muslim lives his earthly life versus how a Christian lives his?

6. The author writes, "Muslims are won to the true Christ the same way most other human beings are—not by argument but by love." Would you agree? Give examples from your own experience or from the experiences of others.

CHAPTER 5:
Not All Texts Are Created Equal

1. What strikes you about the various passages of the Koran the author quotes throughout this chapter? How do you find them similar to the Bible? How do you find them different?

2. At the beginning of the chapter, the author cites a number of important Bible passages. Which two or three passages would you include at the top of your list and why? (You may cite others besides those the author mentions.) Would any of these be particularly helpful when talking to a Muslim friend or acquaintance about the Christian faith?

3. The Koran offers more structure and direction for those who choose to read it systematically than the Bible does. Comment

on this, especially from the perspective of Muslim and Christian Scripture reading habits you may be aware of. Does such structure and direction appeal to you? Would you be likely to read the Bible more regularly if you knew *what* to read *when*?

4. With the exception of one, every sura or chapter of the Koran begins with the phrase, "In the name of God, the merciful, the compassionate." Given the fact that devout Muslims repeat these words many times a day, how do you think they might be affected by them? How might this sentiment affect their worldview? Their view of suffering? Can you think of any equivalent phrase in the Christian faith?

5. Discuss the author's observation that only the opening sura of the Koran is a prayer directed *to* Allah while the remaining 113 are Allah's words to Muhammad, the Muslim community, or humanity at large. Contrast that with greater percentage of the Bible that records human beings talking to God. Does that tell you anything about the difference between Islam and Christianity?

6. The author quotes from Sura 2, the Chapter of the Cow: "On no soul does God place a burden greater than it can bear. It gets every good that it earns, and it suffers every ill that it gets." In some ways, it sounds strikingly like 1 Corinthians 10:13 (God does not tempt us beyond what we can bear), and the theology seems akin to that taught in Galatians 6:6–8 (we reap what we sow). Using this example, are you apt to agree with the idea that all truth is God's truth? Why or why not? Also talk about the concepts of justice and mercy and where they originate.

CHAPTER 6:
Is Allah a False God?

1. The author points out that the God of the Bible and the God of the Koran share much in common, not least because Muhammad

derived much of his understanding from Jewish and Christian sources. How might this be used as a positive in faith conversations with Muslim friends and acquaintances?

2. Likewise, the author notes that there are many significant differences between Christian and Muslim portraits of God. Talk about the Koran's teaching that God is not truly knowable and how that might affect the Muslim mindset. How does the Christian view differ? How should that affect our mindset?

3. Discuss the following statement by the author: "Since the all-powerful Allah needs nothing outside himself, he loves nothing outside himself. Ultimate transcendence prohibits relational nearness." Contrast this with biblical portraits of God as Lover, Good Shepherd, Father, and Savior. Contrast too the solitary unity of the God of Islam with the relational tri-unity (Father, Son, Spirit) of the God of Christianity.

4. Under Islam the best human beings can hope for is to be recognized and rewarded as faithful servants. What might the implications be for an individual who is welcomed into the family of God as a servant on the periphery of the estate versus one welcomed as a beloved child into the Father's house?

5. The author talks about the fatalistic attitude so prevalent in Muslim lands, characterized by the common response to calamity, "What can one do?" Contrast this sense of hopelessness with the repeated message of hope in the Bible. Being sensitive to the turmoil and suffering endured by many Muslims worldwide today, how might you get across this message in your contacts with Muslim friends and acquaintances?

6. Considering the passages presented in the chapter, do you agree with the author's stand that Muslims worship the true God in ignorance rather than pursue a false god? Why or why not?

CHAPTER 7 :

Streams in the Desert: Jewish and Christian Sources in the Koran

1. Discuss Christianity's concept of divine inspiration versus Islam's dictation theory of revelation. How does it strike you that God would use a human vessel, frailties and all, to deliver his Word? What does it say to you about God? About his view of us? How do you think the Muslim perspective differs?

2. Compare and contrast the Muslim and Christian interpretations of Genesis 1–3 as presented in this chapter. What conclusions can you draw about both of these major faith systems from the key stories of the creation account?

3. Noah is another individual common to both the Koran and the Bible. Note the similarities in the two accounts and also the differences. What is the significance of the "end of the story" from each faith perspective?

4. Abraham is considered a major figure in both Islam and Christianity. As the author points out, the Koran identifies the message of Islam with the "religion of Abraham" and, like the Bible, calls him the "friend of God." Elaborate on the Muslim view of the patriarch and why you think they are so partial to him.

5. Now discuss the Christian view of Abraham. There is much Scripture you could draw on, but in particular consider the following: Genesis 12:1–9 (Abraham's call), Genesis 15 (God's covenant with him), and Romans 4 and Hebrews 11:8–19 (passages that talk about his faith). How do the Christian and Muslim perspectives of Abraham differ?

6. Given that the Koran and the Bible share a number of Old Testament accounts (more about this in the next chapter), how do you think you might use such commonalities when witnessing to a Muslim friend or acquaintance? How might you deal with issues related to what the Koran omits or adds to these accounts?

CHAPTER 8:

More Streams in the Desert: Biblical Persons in the Koran

1. Of all the biblical prophets, Muhammad most identified himself with Moses. Why do you think this is so?

2. According to the author, the Koran mentions the giving of the tablets of the law to Moses but reveals nothing of their contents. Based on what you know or have learned thus far about Islam, what might you imagine a Muslim's reaction to the Ten Commandments to be? How might you use the commandments as a springboard to the gospel?

3. Why do you think Muhammad might have written much more about Solomon than he did about David?

4. The author writes, "Other than significant references to Mary and Jesus, the Koran is almost silent on the people and events of the Gospels and early church." What are some reasons why Muhammad likely "dropped" the biblical account at this point?

5. How does the jumbled nature of many of the Koran's accounts to parallel accounts in the Bible affect issues of historicity and inspiration?

6. As the chapter ends, the author conjectures how Muhammad's life and message (and world history) might have changed had he been able to read Greek or Syriac or Latin and had access to the Bible for himself. Picture Muhammad as a contemporary seeker. How would you build on his current knowledge and desires to lead him closer to a place of decision about Jesus Christ?

CHAPTER 9:
The Agony and the Ecstasy: Hell and Heaven

1. Compare and contrast the Muslim and Christian views of divine judgment. How do you think this generally common ground

could be a positive when conversing with a Muslim friend or acquaintance about spiritual things?

2. Muslims typically have a deep uncertainty about their eternal destiny, and even the most devout follower answers, "If God is willing," when asked whether he or she feels sure of reaching Paradise. Contrast this with the concept of eternal security shared by most Christians. How do you think this difference might affect how a person lives day to day?

3. Despite being taught nowhere in the Koran, Islamic tradition says on the day of judgment Muhammad will step forward to act as intercessor for all Muslims, assuming a role that Adam, Noah, Abraham, Moses, and Jesus himself will have declined. Why do you suppose such a tradition has come along? What does it mean to you to know that the Bible teaches that Jesus is our intercessor (see Rom. 8:34; Heb. 7:25)?

4. Like the Christian Scriptures, the Koran depicts hell as a real place. What other similarities do you note? What differences? Comment also on the seven levels of hell and those assigned to each. Note particularly the levels assigned to Christians, Jews, and apostates; why you think they have been "assigned" as they have.

5. Now compare and contrast the Muslim and Christian views of heaven or Paradise. Based on what you have learned in this chapter, put yourself in the place of a Muslim woman and talk about the appeal the afterlife holds for you. Would you imagine a Muslim woman to be more receptive to the gospel than a Muslim man? How would you deal with this issue in interactions with a Muslim of either gender?

6. The author points out that Allah is strangely absent from the Muslim Paradise. What are the implications of an eternity where God is *above* heaven and his creation versus one where he is at

the *center* of it (see Rev. 21–22)? What particularly appeals to you about the biblical teaching?

CHAPTER 10:
What Is the Path of *Jihad*?

1. Respond to the moderate Muslim claim that it is no fairer to judge Islam by extremists and political aberrations than it would be to judge Christianity as a whole because of the Crusades, the Spanish Inquisition, and the Puritan witch hunts. What are your tactics when someone you know attacks Christianity for past or present infractions?

2. The author notes that the Muslim idea of *jihad* of the heart (what Muhammad called "*jihad* against the desires") is roughly parallel to the Christian teaching to put to death the sinful nature, albeit without the aid of the Holy Spirit. Read Romans 7:18–8:17 and talk about how you might use this passage as a springboard in a spiritual conversation with a Muslim friend or acquaintance.

3. *Jihad* of the sword is obviously the most severe striving against evil commanded in the Koran. Discuss the development of this concept as described by the author. Why you think it is often practiced in its most militaristic form today? Based on what you have learned about Muhammad, do you believe he would have envisioned or approved of such an event as the 9/11 attack? Why or why not?

4. The author points out what he believes are vital differences between the Koran's teaching and Old Testament accounts in which God commanded violence. Do you agree or disagree with the author's argument? Why or why not?

5. Following up on the discussion of the previous question, what is your opinion on the concept of "just war"? Would you consider

your opinion consistent with biblical teaching or simply a personal or cultural perspective? Considering the wars the United States has been involved in, from its inception right up to the present, have any (or all) of them been "just wars"? Defend (peacefully!) your opinion.

6. Jesus is called the Prince of Peace (Isa. 9:6), and peace seems to be the consistent message in the Gospels as well as in the New Testament letters. Using a Bible concordance, find the word "peace," then look up and read a few verses that promote a peace-making lifestyle, whether with our "enemies" or within our own family. Also read Jesus' seemingly contradictory words in Matthew 10:34–35 ("I did not come to bring peace, but a sword"). How do you think this particular statement fits with the rest of his message?

EPILOGUE:
The Risk of Ignorance

1. Of the five reasons the author gives for the steady growth of Islam in the West, which one or two seem most critical to you and why? If you know of people who have converted to Islam, why do you think the Muslim faith appeals to them?

2. The author writes, "As Christian denominations have squabbled over relatively petty issues, divided over traditional moral absolutes, and substituted a nondescript ethic of tolerance for the strong meat of the gospel, Islam has stormed into the public arena with a clear, self-confident worldview and a message from the Koran unhampered by cultural compromise." Where specifically have you sensed "waffling" within the church, and how have you been personally influenced by it?

3. If, like many Muslims, Christians in the Western church were to express more passion and commitment, what would that look like? How might it be more obvious in your own life?

4. Do you agree with the author's points about why so many African Americans have been drawn to Islam? Why or why not? What is your reaction to the author's claim that "the American church has all too often failed to make crystal clear by its proclamation and lifestyle that the gospel of Jesus Christ is good news for people of *all races, ethnic groups, and social standings*"?

5. The author notes that the reading of the Sermon on the Mount (Matthew 5–7) has been the catalyst for bringing many Muslims to Jesus Christ. Review these chapters and discuss why you think this passage speaks so powerfully to Muslims.

6. Upon finishing this book, what things stand out to you about Islam, the Koran, and Muhammad that you never before realized? How do you plan to incorporate what you've learned in becoming more spiritually sensitive to Muslims in your midst?

Chapter 1: The Koran through Muslim Eyes

1. Throughout this book I am using the Anglicized form "Koran" since it is the most commonly used spelling by English speakers even though the best technical term is "Qur³an."

2. The Arabic term *Hadith* literally means "a message" or "communication" and refers corporately or individually to the records of Muhammad's actions, conversations, and decrees gathered by his followers in the first two hundred years after the prophet's death. Many of these traditions are not reliable, but the Muslim community generally recognizes six collections to be relatively reliable and thus authoritative for Muslim faith and practice, second only to the Koran. Of these six, the Hadith of al-Bukhari is perhaps best known.

Chapter 2: Where Did the Koran Come From?

1. Thomas Patrick Hughes, *Dictionary of Islam* (London: W. H. Allen & Co., 1935), 370–71.

2. A "sura" is the word for a chapter in the Koran.

Chapter 3: And the Word Became . . . Paper?

1. Much to Zaid's surprise, he later recalled other verses that he had inadvertently left out after believing that this text was the final piece. See below.

2. Indeed, Ibn Masud omitted the opening sura, the Fatiha, from his collection, as well as the last two suras found in all Korans today. The omission of the Fatiha is especially significant since this chapter is the most often quoted Koranic text in the life of the orthodox Muslim. Presumably, these three suras were discarded because the speaker of these words is the believer rather than Allah. Since the Koran is supposed to be the words of Allah directly, this material would not have qualified and so should not have been gathered into the book of Allah's revelations. However, this viewpoint did not prevail, and Suras 1, 113, and 114 are found in every copy of the Koran since the execution of Uthman's decree in the mid-600s.

3. Those interested in detailed lists of these variants should consult the work of Arthur Jeffery, *Materials for the History of the Text of the Qurʾan* (New York: AMS Press, 1975 (1937)), who draws on the books of three Muslim scholars from the tenth and eleventh centuries that sought to compare the received text of Uthman (through Zaid) to those of others detailed in the Hadith.

4. While these variations in dialect and reading do not by and large significantly alter the meaning of the text, they underscore the precariousness of Islam's claim to have the original, pure, and unchanged Word of God.

Chapter 6: Is Allah a False God?

1. *I Dared to Call Him Father* (Waco, TX: Chosen Books, 1978).
2. Ibid., 41–42.

Chapter 7: Streams in the Desert: Jewish and Christian Sources in the Koran

1. It is true that the New Testament calls Noah "a preacher of righteousness" in 2 Peter 2:5, who by his faith (in obediently building the ark) condemned the world (Heb. 11:7). Yet even here there are no clear details of Noah's conversational interactions with his contemporaries. The implication is that Noah preached and condemned through his obedient actions more than through words.

2. Sura 9:114 makes clear that Abraham's prayer was offered only because of a promise he had made to his father. Once it was clear that his father was an enemy of true Islam, Abraham dissociated himself from his

father and refused to pray any longer for him. How different from the spirit of the gospel, where Christ commands his people to pray not only for loved ones but even for enemies and those who persecute the people of God, seeking their salvation!

3. The primary source for this tale is most likely a Jewish rabbinic story traceable to the second century A.D. It can be found in Genesis Rabbah (Noach) 38.11–13 (pp. 310–11 in the Socino edition, ed. Freedman and Simon [London: Socino Press]).

4. According to the Bible, Abraham's father's name was Terah. It is entirely possible that Muhammad heard from others the name of Abraham's servant (identified as Eliezer in Genesis) as Azar (a shortened form), and used it mistakenly of Abraham's father.

5. See Genesis 18:12–15 and 21:1–7, where the name Isaac ("he laughs") is linked with Sarah's laughter at God's doing the impossible and providing her ongoing laughter in her old age through the gift of a son. The Koran never sees or pursues this connection.

6. Though the Koran is silent as to the identity of this son, Islamic tradition typically recognizes him as Ishmael, in contrast to the Bible's assertion that it was Isaac. For the coherence of the overarching biblical narrative, the son to be sacrificed must be Isaac, for he is the child of promise through whom God guaranteed to Abraham a rich lineage. The challenge of faith to Abraham is not only one of trusting God's goodness toward him and his son, but also of trusting that God will somehow still keep his massive promise concerning countless descendants through Abraham and Sarah should Isaac be taken away from them. Islam, however, is not concerned with salvation history as found in the Bible and so puts Ishmael in the place of Isaac, for at least two reasons. (1) Ishmael is the son of Abraham through whom the Arab peoples largely trace their lineage back to the primary patriarch. Thus, he occupies pride of place in Muslim minds. (2) Perhaps more important, immediately following the Koran's account of the intended sacrifice comes Allah's declaration that he gave to Abraham "glad tidings of Isaac—a prophet from the righteous" (37:112). It is hard to imagine such a declaration occurring *after* a story involving Isaac as a lad with his father. Thus, most Muslims quite naturally assume that the earlier story must refer to a son already alive before Isaac. This means Ishmael, Abraham's firstborn son through Sarah's handmaiden, Hagar.

Chapter 8: More Streams in the Desert:
Biblical Persons in the Koran

1. In 20:25–35, Moses does not contend with God at this point in the story but simply asks for courage, the gift of eloquence, and the assistance of Aaron.

2. The question of whether the practice of crucifixion was known and applied in Pharonic Egypt needs scholarly investigation.

3. Apparently Muhammad confuses Haman, the enemy of the Jews during Persian times (see the book of Esther), with this Egyptian protagonist, who is given this Persian name from a much later period of history!

4. As-Samiri is not a proper name as the definite article before the hyphen makes clear. Most Muslim scholars understand this term to mean "the Samaritan," but this is problematic since the Samaritans were not constituted as a separate people until after the deportation of the northern tribes of Israel under the Assyrian empire, some five hundred or more years after the golden calf incident.

5. It is possible that Muhammad had heard the New Testament connection between Elijah and John the Baptist, where in accordance with messianic expectations Elijah was expected to return to life as the herald of the imminent Messiah. Some, including Jesus, referred to John the Baptist as a sort of Elijah *redivivus*.

6. Sura 3:39 speaks of John as one who will bear witness to or confirm the Word from Allah. Most scholars take this as a reference pointing to Jesus.

Chapter 9: The Agony and the Ecstasy:
Hell and Heaven

1. This resurrection is extended not only to all humans but to all other creatures: animals, angels, and *jinn*. Humans will be raised in the same condition as they were originally born—naked, barefoot, and uncircumcised.

2. *Jahannum* is a loan word originally from Hebrew (Ge Hinnom = valley of Hinnom) that was Hellenized (Gehenna) before finding its way into Arabic vocabulary. For the Jews, Hinnom became a symbol for hell as the valley outside the walls of Jerusalem that served as the public dump and was regularly marked by fires and fetid smoke. The word *Jahannum* occurs thirty times in the Koran.

3. While some early Koranic passages seem to indicate that some Christians will end up in paradise, the later texts clearly teach that those who remain Christians and Jews (i.e., rejecting Muhammad's message) will be condemned to hell (see 98:6 in particular).

4. While Christians speak of "heaven" in this sense, for Muslims "heaven" refers primarily to that physical creation that is suspended above the earth.

5. Charis Waddy, *The Muslim Mind* (London: Longman, 1976 [1982]), 129.

Chapter 10: What Is the Path of *Jihad*?

1. Interestingly, one-fifth of all booty taken in *jihad* was to be given to Allah, or more precisely to Muhammad as his representative. According to the Koran (8:41), this treasure was to be used for the support of Muhammad's extended family, for orphans, the poor, and the sojourner.

Epilogue: The Risk of Ignorance

1. It is no surprise that time and again the reading of the Sermon on the Mount has been the catalyst for bringing many Muslims to Jesus Christ. They have rightly sensed the truth of the vision of human community that Jesus paints in Matthew 5–7, and they are attracted both by Jesus' uncompromising standards and his authoritative claims. Were the church to live more recognizably by our own Magna Carta found in these three chapters of Scripture, perhaps many more Muslims would be willing to listen carefully to the message we speak.

Subject Index